♋ CANCER PATH

YOUR DAILY 2025 HOROSCOPE GUIDE

AMANDA M CLARKE

Daily Guidance
SERIES

Welcome to The Cancer Path: Your Daily 2025 Horoscope Guide—your personalized companion for navigating the year ahead with intuition and emotional wisdom. Designed specifically for Cancer individuals, this guide offers daily horoscopes and affirmations that align with your nurturing, sensitive, and deeply intuitive nature.

As a Cancerian, you're known for your strong connection to home, family, and emotional security. This guide will provide you with the insights and cosmic guidance you need to nurture those relationships, while also focusing on personal growth, career, and health.

With each day's horoscope, you'll find thoughtful advice to help you make the most of 2025, providing clarity as you embrace both the challenges and opportunities the year will bring.

9 781763 749634

90000

CANCER

June 21 - July 22

2025
Overview

Cancer in 2025
Overview

Cancer, 2025 is a year of emotional growth, stability, and meaningful connections. You'll feel drawn to strengthening your bonds with family and close friends, as well as creating more balance in your personal life. Early in the year, you'll experience a renewed focus on home and relationships, nurturing those around you while also prioritizing self-care.

Career-wise, your intuition will guide you toward new opportunities, especially mid-year, when personal projects or professional advancements come to light. Emotional resilience will be key to handling any challenges that arise.

By the end of 2025, you'll feel more secure and fulfilled, having deepened your connections and found greater balance in both your personal and professional life. Trust your instincts— they'll lead you to success.

Cancer in 2025
Love and Relationships

Cancer, 2025 brings emotional depth and stronger connections in your love life. For those in committed relationships, this year encourages nurturing your bond with patience, open communication, and affection. You'll feel more connected to your partner as you prioritize spending quality time together, building trust and emotional intimacy.

For single Cancerians, this is a year of potential new beginnings. Your natural warmth and caring nature will attract people who appreciate emotional depth, leading to meaningful relationships. Mid-year brings opportunities to meet someone special through social settings or mutual interests.

Family and friendships will also thrive, as you focus on strengthening the emotional bonds that matter most. By year's end, your relationships will feel more fulfilling and harmonious.

Cancer in 2025
Career

Cancer, 2025 is a year of steady progress and new opportunities in your career. Early in the year, your natural intuition and dedication will guide you toward projects or roles that offer emotional fulfillment and financial stability. This is a great time to take on responsibilities that allow you to showcase your skills, especially those involving nurturing or supporting others.

Mid-year may bring opportunities for advancement or career changes that align with your long-term goals. Trust your instincts when making decisions, as your emotional intelligence will help you navigate challenges and seize new opportunities.

By the end of 2025, you'll feel more secure and accomplished in your professional life, having laid the groundwork for continued success. Stay open to growth and trust the journey.

Cancer in 2025
Wealth

Cancer, 2025 is a year to focus on financial stability and long-term planning. Early in the year, you may find opportunities to increase your income, whether through career advancements, side ventures, or smart financial decisions. Your natural caution will serve you well, helping you avoid impulsive spending and make thoughtful choices about saving and investing.

Mid-year is a great time to assess your financial goals and make any necessary adjustments to ensure you're on track for the future. Consider building an emergency fund or exploring low-risk investments that align with your need for security.

By the end of 2025, you'll feel more financially secure, having made decisions that support both your short-term needs and long-term financial stability.

Cancer in 2025
Health

Cancer, 2025 encourages you to focus on both your physical and emotional well-being. Early in the year, you'll feel motivated to establish healthier routines, such as incorporating regular exercise, improving your diet, and making time for self-care. Emotional balance will also be a key focus—practicing mindfulness, meditation, or relaxation techniques will help manage stress.

Mid-year, you may need to pay extra attention to avoiding burnout, especially if you're balancing career, family, and personal life. Remember to take breaks and prioritize rest.

By the end of 2025, you'll feel more balanced and energized, having embraced healthier habits that support both your body and mind. Focus on maintaining a steady routine, and you'll enjoy lasting benefits to your well-being.

Cancer in 2025
Study

Cancer, 2025 is a year of intellectual expansion and personal development. Whether you're pursuing formal education, learning new skills for your career, or diving into personal interests, this is the perfect year to dedicate time to growth and knowledge. Early in the year, establish a structured study routine that allows you to balance learning with other responsibilities.

Mid-year may bring opportunities for hands-on learning or mentorship, helping you deepen your understanding in areas that matter to you. Don't shy away from exploring new subjects or topics that spark your curiosity—your natural intuition will guide you toward valuable insights.

By the end of 2025, your commitment to study will lead to significant intellectual growth, positioning you for future success in both personal and professional areas.

To all the Cancerians,

Your sensitivity, compassion, and deep emotional strength bring warmth and care to the world around you. This book is dedicated to your nurturing spirit, your ability to connect with others, and the way you embrace life's challenges with grace and resilience.

May the stars always guide and protect your kind and gentle heart.

CANCER
DAILY HOROSCOPE

2025

January

2025

Cancer

1 January 2025

Dear Cancerian, today's energy supports new beginnings. You may feel a surge of motivation to set goals for the year ahead. Trust your intuition as you define your plans, and don't hesitate to dream big. Reflect on your emotional well-being, and seek balance in your personal and professional life. Today is a good time to connect with loved ones and strengthen your support system, as this will help you throughout the year.

Affirmation & Gratitude

I embrace new beginnings with confidence, knowing I have the strength and intuition to achieve my goals.

Cancer

2 January 2025

Dear Cancerian, focus on your relationships today. The cosmos encourages you to deepen emotional connections with those you love. Meaningful conversations and acts of kindness will strengthen your bonds. Be open to expressing your feelings and let others know how much they mean to you. It's also a good day to practice self-care, ensuring that you're emotionally balanced and centered.

Affirmation & Gratitude

I nurture my relationships with love, honesty, and gratitude, creating deeper emotional connections with those I care about.

Cancer

3 January 2025

Dear Cancerian, career growth takes the spotlight today. The energy supports making bold moves toward your professional aspirations. Whether you're seeking new responsibilities or considering new opportunities, today's energy favors proactive steps. Stay focused on your long-term goals and trust that your dedication will pay off. You have the ability to make progress, so stay confident and take initiative.

Affirmation & Gratitude

I trust in my hard work and skills, knowing they will lead me to success and fulfillment.

Cancer

4 January 2025

Dear Cancerian, today, financial planning takes priority. It's a good time to reassess your budget and ensure your goals align with your future aspirations. Make thoughtful decisions that bring long-term stability. Practicality and careful consideration will benefit you, so take time to review any ongoing financial commitments or investment opportunities.

Affirmation & Gratitude

I make responsible financial decisions that ensure peace, stability, and security for my future.

Cancer

5 January 2025

Dear Cancerian, creativity is heightened today. Whether it's working on personal projects or exploring new ideas, today's energy encourages artistic expression. Let your imagination flow, and don't hesitate to try something new. Creativity will bring you joy and fulfillment, so make space in your day to explore your artistic side.

Affirmation & Gratitude

I embrace creativity in all its forms, knowing it brings joy and fulfillment into my life.

Cancer

6 January 2025

Dear Cancerian, today is about self-care and emotional balance. Take time to check in with yourself and address any stress or worries. The cosmos encourages you to rest and recharge. Engage in activities that bring you peace and comfort, and be gentle with yourself. Connecting with nature or practicing mindfulness can help restore your inner harmony.

Affirmation & Gratitude

I prioritize my well-being, knowing that nurturing myself brings peace and balance into my life.

Cancer

7 January 2025

Dear Cancerian, relationships take the spotlight today. You may feel more sensitive to the needs of others, and today's energy encourages you to offer support and care to loved ones. Meaningful conversations will deepen your connections, so be open to listening and understanding. This is also a good day to resolve any lingering misunderstandings.

Affirmation & Gratitude

I nurture my relationships with love, empathy, and honesty, creating deeper bonds with those I care about.

Cancer

8 January 2025

Dear Cancerian, career growth is supported today. The cosmos encourages you to stay focused on your long-term professional goals. You may encounter opportunities to take on new responsibilities or expand your role. Be proactive and trust in your abilities. Your hard work and dedication will be recognized, so keep pushing forward with confidence.

Affirmation & Gratitude

I trust in my hard work and skills, knowing they will lead me to career success.

Cancer

9 January 2025

Dear Cancerian, today is about financial clarity. Take time to reassess your budget and ensure your spending habits align with your goals. Today's energy supports practical financial decisions. Consider seeking advice if needed, but trust your instincts when making choices about your financial future.

Affirmation & Gratitude

I make responsible financial decisions that bring peace and stability into my life.

Cancer

10 January 2025

Dear Cancerian, creativity flows effortlessly today. Whether you're exploring a new hobby or refining an existing project, today's energy supports artistic expression. Let your imagination guide you, and don't be afraid to think outside the box. Creative endeavors will bring fulfillment and joy.

Affirmation & Gratitude

I embrace creativity in all its forms, knowing it enriches my life with joy and purpose.

Cancer

11 January 2025

Dear Cancerian, today focuses on emotional well-being and self-reflection. The cosmos encourages you to take a step back and evaluate your emotional needs. It's important to recognize areas of imbalance and address them. Don't hesitate to seek support from trusted loved ones if you need to talk through your feelings.

Affirmation & Gratitude

I honor my emotions, recognizing that self-care and reflection bring healing and balance to my life.

Cancer

12 January 2025

Dear Cancerian, relationships are highlighted today. Take time to nurture your connections and express your appreciation to those who matter most. Honest and heartfelt communication will strengthen your bonds. Be open to receiving love and support from others, as it will uplift your spirit.

Affirmation & Gratitude

I nurture my relationships with love, gratitude, and kindness, creating deeper emotional connections.

Cancer

13 January 2025

Dear Cancerian, career opportunities may arise today, so stay alert for signs that push you toward growth. Whether you're seeking a promotion or looking for new challenges, today's energy supports forward movement. Take decisive steps toward your goals and trust in your professional journey.

Affirmation & Gratitude

I trust in my skills and dedication, knowing they will lead me to career success and fulfillment.

Cancer

14 January 2025

Dear Cancerian, financial decisions take priority today. The cosmos encourages thoughtful planning for future stability. Reassessing your financial goals and commitments will help bring peace of mind. Practicality and responsibility are your allies today.

Affirmation & Gratitude

I make thoughtful financial decisions that bring stability and peace to my future.

Cancer

15 January 2025

Dear Cancerian, today is perfect for creative expression. The energy supports exploring new ideas or refining ongoing artistic projects. Let your imagination flow freely, and embrace your creative side. Doing so will bring joy and personal fulfillment.

Affirmation & Gratitude

I embrace my creativity, knowing it brings joy and fulfillment into my life.

Cancer

16 January 2025

Dear Cancerian, self-care takes center stage today. The cosmos encourages you to slow down and prioritize your well-being. Rest and relaxation are essential for maintaining emotional balance, so make time for activities that help you recharge.

Affirmation & Gratitude

I honor my need for rest and self-care, knowing it brings balance and peace into my life.

Cancer

17 January 2025

Dear Cancerian, relationships benefit from open communication today. Meaningful conversations with loved ones will help resolve misunderstandings and bring clarity to your connections. Be honest, empathetic, and open to hearing the perspectives of others.

Affirmation & Gratitude

I nurture my relationships with honesty, love, and understanding, strengthening my emotional bonds with those I care about.

Cancer

18 January 2025

Dear Cancerian, career opportunities come into focus today. The energy supports taking decisive steps toward your professional goals. Whether you're seeking new challenges or looking to expand your role, today's energy favors bold action. Stay confident in your abilities.

Affirmation & Gratitude

I trust in my hard work and determination, knowing they will lead me to career success.

Cancer

19 January 2025

Dear Cancerian, financial planning is key today. The cosmos encourages you to reassess your budget and ensure your long-term goals are aligned. Make thoughtful choices that support future stability.

Affirmation & Gratitude

I make responsible financial decisions that bring peace and security into my life.

Cancer

20 January 2025

Dear Cancerian, creativity is heightened today, offering a wonderful opportunity to explore new artistic projects or hobbies. Let your imagination run wild and enjoy the creative process.

Affirmation & Gratitude

I trust in my creativity, knowing it enriches my life and brings joy and fulfillment.

Cancer

21 January 2025

Dear Cancerian, self-care and emotional balance are important today. Take time to reflect on your inner needs and address any feelings of overwhelm. Today is about finding peace and restoring harmony within yourself.

Affirmation & Gratitude

I prioritize my emotional well-being, knowing that self-care brings peace and balance into my life.

Cancer

22 January 2025

Dear Cancerian, relationships are highlighted today. The cosmos encourages deepening emotional bonds with loved ones. Meaningful conversations and shared experiences will strengthen your connections. Be open, honest, and empathetic.

Affirmation & Gratitude

I nurture my relationships with love, gratitude, and kindness, creating deeper emotional connections.

Cancer

23 January 2025

Dear Cancerian, career growth is in the spotlight today. The energy supports making bold moves toward your professional goals. Stay dedicated, and trust in your abilities to succeed.

Affirmation & Gratitude

I trust in my hard work and dedication, knowing they will lead me to career success.

Cancer

24 January 2025

Dear Cancerian, financial planning takes priority today. Reassess your goals and ensure your decisions align with your long-term aspirations. Practical planning now will bring future peace of mind.

Affirmation & Gratitude

I make thoughtful financial decisions that ensure peace and stability for my future.

Cancer

25 January 2025

Dear Cancerian, creativity flows effortlessly today. Explore new ideas or refine ongoing projects. Bold, imaginative thinking will lead to exciting breakthroughs in both personal and professional pursuits.

Affirmation & Gratitude

I embrace creativity in all its forms, knowing it brings joy and fulfillment into my life.

Cancer

26 January 2025

Dear Cancerian, relationships are at the forefront today. Focus on building deeper emotional connections with loved ones through honest and meaningful conversations. Be present and open to understanding others.

Affirmation & Gratitude

I nurture my relationships with love, empathy, and gratitude, creating stronger emotional bonds.

Cancer

27 January 2025

Dear Cancerian, career advancement is possible today. The energy supports taking decisive steps toward your goals. Trust in your skills and take initiative to pursue new opportunities.

Affirmation & Gratitude

I trust in my dedication and abilities to lead me toward success in my career.

Cancer

28 January 2025

Dear Cancerian, financial clarity is key today. Reassessing your budget and future goals will help ensure long-term stability. Make thoughtful decisions that support your financial security.

Affirmation & Gratitude

I make responsible financial decisions that bring peace, stability, and security into my life.

Cancer

29 January 2025

Dear Cancerian, creativity is heightened today. It's a great time to explore new artistic ideas or refine ongoing projects. Your imagination will lead you to exciting possibilities.

Affirmation & Gratitude

I trust in my creativity to bring joy and new opportunities into my life.

Cancer

30 January 2025

Dear Cancerian, relationships benefit from open, honest communication today. Take time to connect with loved ones and express your feelings. Meaningful conversations will strengthen your bonds.

Affirmation & Gratitude

I nurture my relationships with love, honesty, and empathy, fostering deeper emotional connections.

Cancer

31 January 2025

Dear Cancerian, career progress is in focus today. The cosmos encourages bold steps toward your professional aspirations. Stay confident and proactive in pursuing new opportunities.

Affirmation & Gratitude

I trust in my hard work and dedication, knowing they will lead me to success and fulfillment in my career.

February

2025

Cancer

1 February 2025

Dear Cancerian, today's energy favors emotional healing and self-care. Take time to nurture your emotional well-being. Reflect on any lingering feelings or unresolved issues, and seek ways to heal. Whether through meditation, journaling, or simply spending time with loved ones, focus on activities that bring peace.

Affirmation & Gratitude

I honor my emotional needs, knowing that self-care brings peace and healing to my life.

Cancer

2 February 2025

Dear Cancerian, relationships take focus today. The cosmos encourages you to nurture your connections and express your feelings to loved ones. Heartfelt communication will deepen your emotional bonds. Be open, empathetic, and willing to listen. Today is a good day to resolve any misunderstandings.

Affirmation & Gratitude

I nurture my relationships with love, honesty, and empathy, creating deeper emotional bonds.

Cancer

3 February 2025

Dear Cancerian, career growth is highlighted today. The energy supports taking proactive steps toward your professional goals. Whether you're seeking new responsibilities or exploring new opportunities, today's energy favors bold action. Stay confident and trust in your abilities.

Affirmation & Gratitude

I trust in my hard work and dedication, knowing they will lead me to career success.

Cancer

4 February 2025

Dear Cancerian, financial decisions take priority today. Reassessing your budget and long-term goals will bring clarity and peace of mind. Today's energy favors practical financial planning. Take the time to ensure your decisions align with your aspirations.

Affirmation & Gratitude

I make responsible financial decisions that bring peace and security into my life.

Cancer

5 February 2025

Dear Cancerian, creativity flows effortlessly today, making it an excellent time to explore new artistic projects or refine ongoing ideas. Let your imagination guide you, and embrace bold, innovative thinking. Creative expression will bring joy and fulfillment.

Affirmation & Gratitude

I embrace my creativity, knowing it brings joy and fulfillment into my life.

Cancer

6 February 2025

Dear Cancerian, relationships are highlighted today. Focus on deepening your emotional connections with loved ones through meaningful conversations. Be open, empathetic, and understanding in your interactions. Your support and kindness will strengthen your bonds.

Affirmation & Gratitude

I nurture my relationships with love, gratitude, and kindness, creating deeper emotional connections.

Cancer

7 February 2025

Dear Cancerian, career opportunities come into focus today. The energy supports making bold, proactive moves toward your professional goals. Whether you're seeking new challenges or expanding your role, today's energy favors action. Stay grounded and confident in your abilities.

Affirmation & Gratitude

I trust in my skills and hard work to guide me toward professional success.

Cancer

8 February 2025

Dear Cancerian, financial planning takes center stage today. Reassessing your savings and investments will help ensure future stability. Practicality and thoughtful decision-making will bring peace of mind. Take time to review your long-term financial goals.

Affirmation & Gratitude

I make responsible financial decisions that bring stability and peace to my future.

Cancer

9 February 2025

Dear Cancerian, creativity is heightened today, offering a great opportunity to explore new artistic ideas or hobbies. Let your imagination flow freely, and don't hesitate to try something new. Creative expression will bring joy.

Affirmation & Gratitude

I trust in my creativity, knowing it brings new opportunities and fulfillment into my life.

Cancer

10 February 2025

Dear Cancerian, relationships take focus today. The cosmos encourages you to nurture your emotional bonds with loved ones. Meaningful conversations and shared experiences will deepen your connections. Be open, empathetic, and willing to listen.

Affirmation & Gratitude

I nurture my relationships with love, honesty, and empathy, creating stronger emotional bonds.

Cancer

11 February 2025

Dear Cancerian, career growth is supported today. The cosmos encourages you to take decisive steps toward your professional goals. Whether it's seeking a new opportunity or expanding your role, today's energy supports forward movement. Stay confident and proactive in your actions.

Affirmation & Gratitude

I trust in my hard work and dedication, knowing they will lead me to career success.

Cancer

12 February 2025

Dear Cancerian, financial decisions take priority today. Reassessing your budget and aligning your spending habits with your goals will bring clarity. Make thoughtful choices that support long-term security.

Affirmation & Gratitude

I make responsible financial decisions that ensure peace, stability, and security in my life.

Cancer

13 February 2025

Dear Cancerian, creativity is heightened today, making it a perfect time to dive into artistic projects or hobbies. Let your imagination guide you and embrace the creative process without hesitation.

Affirmation & Gratitude

I embrace my creativity, knowing it brings joy and fulfillment into my life.

Cancer

14 February 2025

Dear Cancerian, relationships are highlighted today, and the cosmos encourages open communication with loved ones. Meaningful conversations and acts of kindness will strengthen your emotional bonds. Be honest and empathetic.

Affirmation & Gratitude

I nurture my relationships with love, honesty, and gratitude, fostering deeper connections with those I care about.

Cancer

15 February 2025

Dear Cancerian, career opportunities may arise today. The energy supports making bold moves toward your goals. Whether it's seeking a promotion or taking on new challenges, trust in your abilities and take action.

Affirmation & Gratitude

I trust in my skills and hard work to guide me toward success and fulfillment in my career.

Cancer

16 February 2025

Dear Cancerian, financial planning is important today. Reassessing your financial commitments and goals will bring clarity and help ensure future stability. Make practical decisions that align with your aspirations.

Affirmation & Gratitude

I make thoughtful financial decisions that ensure stability and peace of mind for my future.

Cancer

17 February 2025

Dear Cancerian, creativity flows effortlessly today, making it an ideal time to explore new artistic ventures or refine ongoing projects. Let your imagination lead the way, and enjoy the creative process.

Affirmation & Gratitude

I trust in my creativity to open doors to new opportunities and fulfillment.

Cancer

18 February 2025

Dear Cancerian, relationships take focus today. The cosmos encourages nurturing emotional bonds with loved ones. Honest communication and shared experiences will deepen your connections. Be present and empathetic in your interactions.

Affirmation & Gratitude

I nurture my relationships with love, honesty, and gratitude, creating deep emotional bonds with those I cherish.

Cancer

19 February 2025

Dear Cancerian, career growth is highlighted today. The energy supports taking bold, proactive steps toward your professional goals. Stay grounded and confident as you pursue new opportunities or expand your role.

Affirmation & Gratitude

I trust in my hard work and dedication to guide me toward success and personal growth.

Cancer

20 February 2025

Dear Cancerian, financial decisions are key today. Reassessing your long-term goals and ensuring your financial plans align with them will bring peace of mind. Practicality is your ally today.

Affirmation & Gratitude

I make responsible financial decisions that ensure stability and security for my future.

Cancer

21 February 2025

Dear Cancerian, creativity is heightened today, offering a perfect opportunity to explore new ideas or artistic projects. Let your imagination flow freely and embrace bold, innovative thinking.

Affirmation & Gratitude

I trust in my creativity to bring joy and new possibilities into my life.

Cancer

22 February 2025

Dear Cancerian, relationships take priority today, with opportunities to deepen emotional bonds with loved ones. Meaningful conversations and acts of kindness will strengthen your connections.

Affirmation & Gratitude

I nurture my relationships with love, empathy, and gratitude, creating deeper emotional connections.

Cancer

23 February 2025

Dear Cancerian, career progress is supported today. The cosmos encourages you to take proactive steps toward your goals. Stay motivated and trust in your abilities to achieve success.

Affirmation & Gratitude

I trust in my skills and hard work to lead me toward career success and fulfillment.

Cancer

24 February 2025

Dear Cancerian, financial planning takes center stage today. Reassessing your budget and aligning your financial goals with your future aspirations will bring clarity and peace.

Affirmation & Gratitude

I make thoughtful financial decisions that ensure stability and peace of mind for my future.

Cancer

25 February 2025

Dear Cancerian, creativity flows effortlessly today, making it a great time to explore new ideas or refine ongoing artistic projects. Let your imagination guide you toward fulfilling outcomes.

Affirmation & Gratitude

I embrace creativity in all its forms, knowing it enriches my life with joy and fulfillment.

Cancer

26 February 2025

Dear Cancerian, relationships are in the spotlight today. The cosmos encourages open communication with loved ones to strengthen your emotional bonds. Be empathetic, patient, and understanding in your interactions.

Affirmation & Gratitude

I nurture my relationships with love, honesty, and gratitude, fostering deeper emotional connections with those I care about.

Cancer

27 February 2025

Dear Cancerian, career advancement is possible today. The energy supports making decisive moves toward your goals. Whether it's a new role or expanding responsibilities, today favors action.

Affirmation & Gratitude

I trust in my hard work and determination to guide me toward success in my career.

Cancer

28 February 2025

Dear Cancerian, financial clarity is key today. Reassessing your goals and making thoughtful financial decisions will ensure long-term stability. Practical choices today will bring future peace.

Affirmation & Gratitude

I make responsible financial decisions that ensure stability and security for my future.

March

2025

Cancer

1 March 2025

Dear Cancerian, today's energy supports self-reflection and emotional balance. Take time to check in with your feelings and ensure you're aligned with your personal goals. Inner peace is key, so spend time nurturing yourself through meditation, journaling, or connecting with loved ones. Today is a good day to focus on emotional healing and letting go of any stress that no longer serves you.

Affirmation & Gratitude

I honor my emotional well-being, knowing that self-care brings peace and balance into my life.

Cancer

2 March 2025

Dear Cancerian, relationships are in focus today, and the cosmos encourages you to express your feelings openly with those you love. Meaningful conversations and shared experiences will strengthen your connections. Be empathetic and kind, as your understanding will help build stronger bonds.

Affirmation & Gratitude

I nurture my relationships with love, honesty, and kindness, creating deep emotional connections with those I care about.

Cancer

3 March 2025

Dear Cancerian, career growth is supported today, and the energy favors taking bold steps toward your professional aspirations. Whether you're considering new opportunities or expanding your current role, stay confident and proactive. Today's energy is perfect for making decisive moves that align with your long-term vision.

Affirmation & Gratitude

I trust in my dedication and skills to guide me toward success and fulfillment in my career.

Cancer

4 March 2025

Dear Cancerian, financial decisions take priority today. Reassessing your budget and long-term goals will help you stay on track. Thoughtful planning and responsible choices will lead to future security. Take time to reflect on your financial habits and ensure they align with your aspirations.

Affirmation & Gratitude

I make responsible financial decisions that ensure stability and peace in my future.

Cancer

5 March 2025

Dear Cancerian, creativity flows effortlessly today, making it a perfect time to explore new artistic projects or hobbies. Whether you're starting something new or refining an existing idea, let your imagination guide you. Creative expression will bring joy and fulfillment.

Affirmation & Gratitude

I embrace creativity in all its forms, knowing it brings joy and new opportunities into my life.

Cancer

6 March 2025

Dear Cancerian, relationships take focus today, and the cosmos encourages deepening emotional bonds with loved ones. Meaningful conversations and acts of kindness will help strengthen your connections. Be open, empathetic, and willing to listen. Today is a great day to spend quality time with those who matter most.

Affirmation & Gratitude

I nurture my relationships with love, empathy, and gratitude, creating deeper emotional bonds with those I cherish.

Cancer

7 March 2025

Dear Cancerian, career progress is highlighted today. The energy supports taking bold, proactive steps toward your professional goals. Stay motivated and trust that your hard work will be rewarded. Whether it's expanding your role or seeking new opportunities, today's energy favors forward movement.

Affirmation & Gratitude

I trust in my hard work and skills to lead me toward career success and fulfillment.

Cancer

8 March 2025

Dear Cancerian, financial planning takes priority today. Reassessing your budget and investments will help bring clarity and ensure future stability. Practical decisions today will lead to peace of mind in the future. Take time to review your financial goals and ensure they are aligned with your long-term vision.

Affirmation & Gratitude

I make responsible financial decisions that bring peace, stability, and security into my life.

Cancer

9 March 2025

Dear Cancerian, creativity is heightened today, offering a perfect opportunity to dive into artistic projects or personal hobbies. Let your imagination guide you and don't hesitate to try new ideas. Creative expression will bring joy and satisfaction.

Affirmation & Gratitude

I embrace creativity, knowing it brings fulfillment and new possibilities into my life.

Cancer

10 March 2025

Dear Cancerian, relationships take focus today, and the cosmos encourages open communication with loved ones. Meaningful conversations will strengthen your emotional bonds. Be honest, empathetic, and willing to listen to the needs of others.

Affirmation & Gratitude

I nurture my relationships with love, honesty, and empathy, fostering deeper connections with those I care about.

Cancer

11 March 2025

Dear Cancerian, career growth is in the spotlight today. The energy supports taking bold, proactive steps toward your goals. Whether you're exploring new opportunities or expanding your current role, stay focused and confident in your abilities. Today's energy favors progress and forward movement.

Affirmation & Gratitude

I trust in my skills and hard work to guide me toward professional success and fulfillment.

Cancer

12 March 2025

Dear Cancerian, financial clarity is important today. Take time to reassess your budget and ensure your goals align with your long-term aspirations. Responsible planning will lead to future stability and peace of mind.

Affirmation & Gratitude

I make thoughtful financial decisions that ensure stability and peace in my future.

Cancer

13 March 2025

Dear Cancerian, creativity flows effortlessly today. Whether you're exploring new ideas or refining ongoing projects, today's energy supports imaginative thinking. Let your creativity guide you toward fulfilling outcomes.

Affirmation & Gratitude

I embrace creativity in all its forms, knowing it enriches my life with joy and fulfillment.

Cancer

14 March 2025

Dear Cancerian, relationships take focus today, and the cosmos encourages nurturing emotional connections with loved ones. Meaningful conversations and shared experiences will deepen your bonds. Be present, empathetic, and open to expressing your feelings.

Affirmation & Gratitude

I nurture my relationships with love, honesty, and gratitude, creating deeper emotional connections with those I care about.

Cancer

15 March 2025

Dear Cancerian, career advancement is possible today. The energy supports taking decisive actions toward your professional goals. Whether it's a new role or expanding responsibilities, today favors bold moves. Stay grounded and confident in your abilities.

Affirmation & Gratitude

I trust in my hard work and determination to lead me toward success in my career.

Cancer

16 March 2025

Dear Cancerian, financial decisions take priority today. Reassessing your financial goals and making thoughtful choices will ensure long-term stability. Take time to review your budget and ensure it aligns with your future aspirations.

Affirmation & Gratitude

I make responsible financial decisions that bring stability and peace to my future.

Cancer

17 March 2025

Dear Cancerian, creativity is heightened today, making it a great time to explore new ideas or refine ongoing projects. Let your imagination flow freely, and embrace bold, innovative thinking. Creative expression will bring joy and fulfillment.

Affirmation & Gratitude

I trust in my creativity to open doors to new opportunities and fulfilling experiences.

Cancer

18 March 2025

Dear Cancerian, relationships take focus today, with opportunities to deepen emotional bonds with loved ones. Meaningful conversations will enhance your connections. Be open, kind, and understanding in your interactions.

Affirmation & Gratitude

I nurture my relationships with love, honesty, and empathy, creating deeper emotional connections with those I cherish.

Cancer

19 March 2025

Dear Cancerian, career growth is highlighted today, and the cosmos encourages you to take bold steps toward your goals. Stay proactive and trust in your skills to achieve success.

Affirmation & Gratitude

I trust in my hard work and dedication to guide me toward professional success and fulfillment.

Cancer

20 March 2025

Dear Cancerian, financial planning takes center stage today. Reassessing your long-term goals and ensuring your financial strategies align with them will bring clarity and security. Practical choices today will benefit your future.

Affirmation & Gratitude

I make responsible financial decisions that ensure stability and peace of mind for my future.

Cancer

21 March 2025

Dear Cancerian, creativity flows effortlessly today, offering a perfect opportunity to explore new artistic projects or hobbies. Let your imagination guide you toward new and exciting possibilities.

Affirmation & Gratitude

I embrace creativity in all its forms, knowing it enriches my life and brings fulfillment.

Cancer

22 March 2025

Dear Cancerian, relationships take priority today, with the cosmos encouraging you to deepen emotional bonds with loved ones. Meaningful conversations and shared moments will strengthen your connections. Be empathetic and honest.

Affirmation & Gratitude

I nurture my relationships with love, gratitude, and kindness, creating deep emotional bonds.

Cancer

23 March 2025

Dear Cancerian, career progress is highlighted today. The energy supports taking decisive steps toward your professional goals. Stay focused, motivated, and confident in your abilities to succeed.

Affirmation & Gratitude

I trust in my dedication and hard work to guide me toward career success.

Cancer

24 March 2025

Dear Cancerian, financial clarity is key today. Reassessing your budget and making practical decisions will ensure long-term stability. Responsible choices today will secure your future.

Affirmation & Gratitude

I make thoughtful financial decisions that ensure peace, stability, and security for my future.

Cancer

25 March 2025

Dear Cancerian, creativity is heightened today, making it a great time to explore new artistic projects or refine ongoing ideas. Let your imagination flow freely and enjoy the process.

Affirmation & Gratitude

I trust in my creativity to bring new and fulfilling experiences into my life.

Cancer

26 March 2025

Dear Cancerian, relationships are highlighted today. Focus on building deeper emotional connections with loved ones through honest and open communication. Meaningful conversations will strengthen your bonds.

Affirmation & Gratitude

I nurture my relationships with love, honesty, and empathy, fostering deeper connections with those I care about.

Cancer

27 March 2025

Dear Cancerian, career advancement is possible today. The cosmos encourages taking bold, proactive steps toward your professional goals. Stay grounded, confident, and motivated to reach your aspirations.

Affirmation & Gratitude

I trust in my skills and hard work to guide me toward career success.

Cancer

28 March 2025

Dear Cancerian, financial decisions are important today. Take time to reassess your financial plans and ensure they align with your long-term goals. Practical planning will lead to future security.

Affirmation & Gratitude

I make responsible financial decisions that bring peace, stability, and security into my life.

Cancer

29 March 2025

Dear Cancerian, creativity is heightened today, offering a wonderful opportunity to explore new artistic projects or refine existing ideas. Let your imagination guide you and embrace the creative process.

Affirmation & Gratitude

I embrace creativity in all its forms, knowing it brings joy and fulfillment into my life.

Cancer

30 March 2025

Dear Cancerian, relationships take focus today, with the cosmos encouraging open communication and emotional connections. Meaningful conversations will enhance your bonds with loved ones. Be honest, empathetic, and willing to listen.

Affirmation & Gratitude

I nurture my relationships with love, honesty, and gratitude, creating deeper emotional bonds with those I cherish.

Cancer

31 March 2025

Dear Cancerian, career progress is in the spotlight today, and the energy supports taking bold, decisive steps toward your professional aspirations. Stay motivated, confident, and proactive as you pursue your goals.

Affirmation & Gratitude

I trust in my hard work and skills to lead me toward success and fulfillment in my career.

April

2025

Cancer

1 April 2025

Dear Cancerian, today's energy supports emotional balance and self-care. Take time to nurture your inner peace and reflect on your personal growth. Whether through meditation, journaling, or simply spending quiet moments with yourself, focus on activities that restore your emotional well-being. Today is also a good day to reconnect with loved ones and build on your emotional bonds.

Affirmation & Gratitude

I honor my emotional well-being, knowing that nurturing myself brings peace and balance into my life.

Cancer

2 April 2025

Dear Cancerian, relationships take center stage today, and the cosmos encourages open communication with those you love. Meaningful conversations will strengthen your emotional connections, and your empathy will help you resolve any lingering misunderstandings. Be open to listening and sharing your feelings honestly.

Affirmation & Gratitude

I nurture my relationships with love, honesty, and kindness, creating deeper emotional bonds with those I care about.

Cancer

3 April 2025

Dear Cancerian, career growth is supported today. The energy favors making bold, proactive moves toward your professional goals. Whether you're expanding your role or exploring new opportunities, trust in your abilities and take decisive action. Your dedication will pay off.

Affirmation & Gratitude

I trust in my hard work and skills to lead me to success and fulfillment in my career.

Cancer

4 April 2025

Dear Cancerian, financial planning is key today. Reassessing your budget and long-term goals will bring clarity and peace of mind. Make thoughtful decisions that ensure stability and align with your future aspirations. Today's energy favors practical financial choices.

Affirmation & Gratitude

I make responsible financial decisions that ensure peace, stability, and security in my life.

Cancer

5 April 2025

Dear Cancerian, creativity is heightened today, making it an ideal time to explore new artistic projects or refine ongoing ones. Whether you're working on a hobby or professional venture, let your imagination guide you. Creative expression will bring joy and fulfillment.

Affirmation & Gratitude

I embrace creativity in all its forms, knowing it enriches my life with joy and fulfillment.

Cancer

6 April 2025

Dear Cancerian, relationships take focus today, and the cosmos encourages you to deepen emotional bonds with loved ones. Meaningful conversations and shared moments will enhance your connections. Be present, empathetic, and open to expressing your emotions.

Affirmation & Gratitude

I nurture my relationships with love, empathy, and gratitude, creating deeper emotional connections with those I cherish.

Cancer

7 April 2025

Dear Cancerian, career progress is highlighted today. The energy supports taking bold, decisive steps toward your professional aspirations. Stay confident and proactive in pursuing your goals, knowing that your hard work will lead to positive outcomes.

Affirmation & Gratitude

I trust in my skills and dedication to guide me toward career success and fulfillment.

Cancer

8 April 2025

Dear Cancerian, financial clarity is important today. Reassessing your goals and making thoughtful financial decisions will help ensure future security. Today's energy supports practical planning that brings peace of mind. Take time to review your financial commitments.

Affirmation & Gratitude

I make responsible financial decisions that bring peace, stability, and security into my life.

Cancer

9 April 2025

Dear Cancerian, creativity flows effortlessly today, offering a perfect opportunity to explore new ideas or refine ongoing projects. Let your imagination lead you toward fulfilling outcomes, whether in your personal or professional endeavors.

Affirmation & Gratitude

I trust in my creativity to bring new and exciting opportunities into my life.

Cancer

10 April 2025

Dear Cancerian, relationships take focus today, with opportunities to deepen emotional connections through open and honest communication. Be kind, empathetic, and willing to listen, as meaningful conversations will strengthen your bonds.

Affirmation & Gratitude

I nurture my relationships with love, honesty, and empathy, fostering deeper emotional connections with those I care about.

Cancer

11 April 2025

Dear Cancerian, career growth is highlighted today, and the energy supports making bold moves toward your professional goals. Stay focused on your long-term aspirations, and don't hesitate to take action on opportunities that come your way. Trust in your abilities and maintain confidence as you navigate your career path.

Affirmation & Gratitude

I trust in my hard work and dedication, knowing they will lead me to career success.

Cancer

12 April 2025

Dear Cancerian, financial decisions take priority today. Reassessing your budget and ensuring that your financial goals align with your future aspirations will bring clarity. Make thoughtful choices that ensure long-term stability and peace of mind.

Affirmation & Gratitude

I make responsible financial decisions that ensure peace, stability, and security for my future.

Cancer

13 April 2025

Dear Cancerian, creativity flows effortlessly today. Whether you're working on artistic projects or exploring new hobbies, today's energy supports bold thinking and imaginative solutions. Let your creativity lead the way and enjoy the process.

Affirmation & Gratitude

I embrace my creativity, knowing it brings joy and new opportunities into my life.

Cancer

14 April 2025

Dear Cancerian, relationships are highlighted today. The cosmos encourages nurturing your emotional connections with loved ones through open, honest communication. Meaningful conversations will deepen your bonds and bring clarity to any unresolved issues. Be empathetic and kind in your interactions.

Affirmation & Gratitude

I nurture my relationships with love, honesty, and gratitude, creating deeper emotional bonds with those I care about.

Cancer

15 April 2025

Dear Cancerian, career advancement is possible today, and the energy supports taking bold, decisive steps toward your goals. Stay grounded and confident in your abilities as you pursue new opportunities or expand your current role.

Affirmation & Gratitude

I trust in my hard work and skills to guide me toward success and fulfillment in my career.

Cancer

16 April 2025

Dear Cancerian, financial planning takes focus today. Reassessing your long-term goals and making practical decisions will ensure future stability. Take time to review your financial plans and align them with your future aspirations.

Affirmation & Gratitude

I make thoughtful financial decisions that bring stability and peace of mind for my future.

Cancer

17 April 2025

Dear Cancerian, creativity is heightened today, offering a great opportunity to explore new artistic projects or refine ongoing ones. Let your imagination guide you and embrace the creative process fully.

Affirmation & Gratitude

I trust in my creativity to bring joy and new possibilities into my life.

Cancer

18 April 2025

Dear Cancerian, relationships take priority today, with the cosmos encouraging open communication with loved ones. Meaningful conversations will deepen your emotional bonds and bring clarity to any lingering misunderstandings. Be present, empathetic, and understanding.

Affirmation & Gratitude

I nurture my relationships with love, empathy, and kindness, creating deeper connections with those I care about.

Cancer

19 April 2025

Dear Cancerian, career progress is supported today. The energy favors taking proactive steps toward your professional aspirations. Whether you're expanding your responsibilities or seeking new challenges, stay focused and confident in your abilities.

Affirmation & Gratitude

I trust in my skills and dedication to guide me toward career success and fulfillment.

Cancer

20 April 2025

Dear Cancerian, financial clarity is important today. Reassessing your financial strategies and ensuring they align with your long-term goals will bring peace of mind. Practical planning today will secure future stability.

Affirmation & Gratitude

I make responsible financial decisions that ensure peace, stability, and security for my future.

Cancer

21 April 2025

Dear Cancerian, creativity is heightened today, making it a great time to dive into new ideas or artistic projects. Whether you're starting something new or refining an ongoing project, let your imagination guide you.

Affirmation & Gratitude

I embrace creativity in all its forms, knowing it brings joy and fulfillment into my life.

Cancer

22 April 2025

Dear Cancerian, relationships take focus today. The cosmos encourages nurturing emotional connections with loved ones through open communication. Be honest, empathetic, and willing to listen, as today's energy favors meaningful conversations that will strengthen your bonds.

Affirmation & Gratitude

I nurture my relationships with love, honesty, and gratitude, fostering deeper emotional connections.

Cancer

23 April 2025

Dear Cancerian, career growth is in the spotlight today. The energy supports taking bold steps toward your professional aspirations. Whether you're seeking new opportunities or expanding your current role, stay motivated and confident in your abilities.

Affirmation & Gratitude

I trust in my dedication and skills to lead me toward career success and fulfillment.

Cancer

24 April 2025

Dear Cancerian, financial planning takes priority today. Reassessing your budget and aligning your goals with your long-term vision will bring clarity. Practical decisions made today will ensure peace of mind in the future.

Affirmation & Gratitude

I make thoughtful financial decisions that ensure stability and peace for my future.

Cancer

25 April 2025

Dear Cancerian, creativity flows effortlessly today, making it a wonderful time to explore new artistic ventures or refine ongoing projects. Let your imagination run wild and enjoy the creative process.

Affirmation & Gratitude

I trust in my creativity to bring new and fulfilling experiences into my life.

Cancer

26 April 2025

Dear Cancerian, relationships are highlighted today, and the cosmos encourages nurturing emotional bonds with loved ones. Meaningful conversations and shared experiences will deepen your connections. Be kind, empathetic, and honest in your interactions.

Affirmation & Gratitude

I nurture my relationships with love, honesty, and empathy, creating deeper emotional connections with those I care about.

Cancer

27 April 2025

Dear Cancerian, career advancement is possible today, and the energy supports taking bold, proactive steps toward your goals. Stay grounded, confident, and motivated as you navigate new challenges and opportunities.

Affirmation & Gratitude

I trust in my hard work and determination to guide me toward success in my career.

Cancer

28 April 2025

Dear Cancerian, financial clarity is key today. Reassessing your budget and making responsible financial decisions will ensure future stability. Practical choices made today will benefit your long-term security.

Affirmation & Gratitude

I make responsible financial decisions that ensure peace, stability, and security for my future.

Cancer

29 April 2025

Dear Cancerian, creativity is heightened today, making it a perfect time to explore new ideas or artistic projects. Whether you're refining an ongoing project or starting something new, let your imagination guide you.

Affirmation & Gratitude

I embrace creativity in all its forms, knowing it enriches my life with joy and fulfillment.

Cancer

30 April 2025

Dear Cancerian, relationships take focus today, with the cosmos encouraging open and honest communication with loved ones. Meaningful conversations will enhance your bonds and bring clarity to any misunderstandings.

Affirmation & Gratitude

I nurture my relationships with love, honesty, and empathy, fostering deeper emotional connections.

May

2025

Cancer

1 May 2025

Dear Cancerian, today's energy supports emotional balance and self-care. Take time to reflect on your personal goals and make sure you're aligned with your inner desires. Nurturing your emotional well-being will bring peace and clarity. Whether it's through mindfulness practices, creative outlets, or spending time with loved ones, focus on what restores your balance.

Affirmation & Gratitude

I honor my emotional well-being, knowing that self-care brings peace and harmony to my life.

Cancer

2 May 2025

Dear Cancerian, relationships take focus today, and the cosmos encourages open and meaningful communication with loved ones. Deep conversations and shared experiences will strengthen your emotional bonds. Be empathetic and willing to listen. It's also a good time to express your appreciation for those you cherish.

Affirmation & Gratitude

I nurture my relationships with love, honesty, and gratitude, creating deeper emotional connections with those I care about.

Cancer

3 May 2025

Dear Cancerian, career growth is highlighted today. The energy supports making bold, proactive moves toward your professional goals. Whether you're expanding your responsibilities or exploring new opportunities, today's energy favors forward movement. Stay grounded and trust in your abilities.

Affirmation & Gratitude

I trust in my hard work and dedication to lead me toward career success and fulfillment.

Cancer

4 May 2025

Dear Cancerian, financial planning is key today. Reassessing your budget and ensuring your goals align with your long-term vision will bring clarity. Today's energy supports practical financial decisions that will ensure peace of mind in the future. Take time to reflect on your financial habits.

Affirmation & Gratitude

I make thoughtful financial decisions that bring stability and peace to my future.

Cancer

5 May 2025

Dear Cancerian, creativity is heightened today. Whether you're exploring new artistic ideas or refining ongoing projects, today's energy supports bold thinking and imagination. Let your creativity flow freely, and embrace the joy of expression.

Affirmation & Gratitude

I embrace creativity in all its forms, knowing it brings joy and new opportunities into my life.

Cancer

6 May 2025

Dear Cancerian, relationships take center stage today. The cosmos encourages nurturing emotional connections with loved ones through open, heartfelt conversations. Be present, empathetic, and honest in your interactions. Today's energy favors strengthening your bonds with those who matter most.

Affirmation & Gratitude

I nurture my relationships with love, honesty, and gratitude, fostering deeper emotional connections with those I cherish.

Cancer

7 May 2025

Dear Cancerian, career progress is in the spotlight today. The energy supports taking bold steps toward your goals. Whether you're expanding your role or seeking new challenges, stay confident and focused on your long-term aspirations.

Affirmation & Gratitude

I trust in my skills and dedication to guide me toward career success and fulfillment.

Cancer

8 May 2025

Dear Cancerian, financial clarity is important today. Reassessing your financial goals and aligning them with your future plans will bring peace of mind. Today's energy supports practical planning for long-term stability and security.

Affirmation & Gratitude

I make responsible financial decisions that ensure peace, stability, and security for my future.

Cancer

9 May 2025

Dear Cancerian, creativity flows effortlessly today, offering a perfect opportunity to explore new artistic ventures or refine ongoing projects. Let your imagination guide you, and embrace the creative process fully.

Affirmation & Gratitude

I trust in my creativity to bring new and fulfilling experiences into my life.

Cancer

10 May 2025

Dear Cancerian, relationships are highlighted today. Meaningful conversations and shared experiences will strengthen your emotional bonds with loved ones. Be empathetic, kind, and open to deepening your connections. Today's energy favors emotional closeness.

Affirmation & Gratitude

I nurture my relationships with love, honesty, and empathy, fostering deeper emotional bonds with those I care about.

Cancer

11 May 2025

Dear Cancerian, career growth is highlighted today. The energy supports taking proactive steps toward your professional goals. Whether you're seeking new opportunities or expanding your current role, today's energy favors forward movement. Trust in your abilities and stay confident.

Affirmation & Gratitude

I trust in my hard work and dedication to lead me toward career success and personal growth.

Cancer

12 May 2025

Dear Cancerian, financial planning is key today. Reassessing your long-term goals and ensuring your financial choices align with them will bring clarity. Practical decisions made today will ensure future stability. Take time to reflect on your financial habits.

Affirmation & Gratitude

I make thoughtful financial decisions that bring stability and peace to my future.

Cancer

13 May 2025

Dear Cancerian, creativity is heightened today. Whether you're exploring new artistic ideas or refining ongoing projects, today's energy supports bold thinking and imagination. Let your creativity flow freely and embrace the joy of expression.

Affirmation & Gratitude

I embrace creativity in all its forms, knowing it enriches my life with joy and fulfillment.

Cancer

14 May 2025

Dear Cancerian, relationships take focus today. The cosmos encourages nurturing your emotional connections with loved ones through open, meaningful conversations. Today's energy favors strengthening bonds and deepening emotional ties with those you cherish.

Affirmation & Gratitude

I nurture my relationships with love, honesty, and gratitude, fostering deeper emotional connections with those I care about.

Cancer

15 May 2025

Dear Cancerian, career progress is in the spotlight today. The energy supports making bold, decisive steps toward your professional aspirations. Whether you're expanding your responsibilities or seeking new challenges, stay focused and confident in your abilities.

Affirmation & Gratitude

I trust in my skills and hard work to guide me toward career success and fulfillment.

Cancer

16 May 2025

Dear Cancerian, financial clarity is important today. Reassessing your budget and aligning your goals with your long-term vision will bring peace of mind. Practical choices made today will ensure future security.

Affirmation & Gratitude

I make responsible financial decisions that ensure peace, stability, and security for my future.

Cancer

17 May 2025

Dear Cancerian, creativity flows effortlessly today, offering a great opportunity to explore new artistic projects or refine ongoing ones. Let your imagination guide you toward fulfilling outcomes. Creative expression will bring joy and personal satisfaction.

Affirmation & Gratitude

I trust in my creativity to bring new and fulfilling experiences into my life.

Cancer

18 May 2025

Dear Cancerian, relationships are highlighted today, and the cosmos encourages you to deepen emotional bonds with loved ones. Meaningful conversations and shared experiences will strengthen your connections. Be kind, empathetic, and open in your interactions.

Affirmation & Gratitude

I nurture my relationships with love, empathy, and gratitude, fostering deeper emotional bonds with those I cherish.

Cancer

19 May 2025

Dear Cancerian, career advancement is possible today. The energy supports taking bold, proactive steps toward your goals. Stay grounded, confident, and motivated to pursue new opportunities or expand your current role.

Affirmation & Gratitude

I trust in my hard work and skills to guide me toward success and fulfillment in my career.

Cancer

20 May 2025

Dear Cancerian, financial clarity is key today. Reassessing your financial strategies and ensuring they align with your long-term goals will bring peace of mind. Practical planning today will benefit your future.

Affirmation & Gratitude

I make thoughtful financial decisions that ensure peace, stability, and security in my life.

Cancer

21 May 2025

Dear Cancerian, creativity is heightened today, making it a perfect time to explore new artistic ideas or refine ongoing projects. Let your imagination guide you and embrace the creative process fully.

Affirmation & Gratitude

I embrace creativity in all its forms, knowing it brings joy and fulfillment into my life.

Cancer

22 May 2025

Dear Cancerian, relationships take focus today, and the cosmos encourages open and honest communication with loved ones. Meaningful conversations will strengthen your emotional bonds and deepen your connections. Be empathetic and willing to listen.

Affirmation & Gratitude

I nurture my relationships with love, honesty, and gratitude, fostering deeper emotional connections with those I care about.

Cancer

23 May 2025

Dear Cancerian, career progress is in the spotlight today. The energy supports taking proactive steps toward your professional goals. Stay motivated, confident, and focused on your long-term vision as you pursue new opportunities.

Affirmation & Gratitude

I trust in my skills and dedication to guide me toward career success and fulfillment.

Cancer

24 May 2025

Dear Cancerian, financial planning takes priority today. Reassessing your budget and long-term goals will bring clarity. Today's energy supports practical financial decisions that will ensure future stability.

Affirmation & Gratitude

I make responsible financial decisions that bring peace, stability, and security into my life.

Cancer

25 May 2025

Dear Cancerian, creativity flows effortlessly today, making it a great time to explore new ideas or artistic projects. Whether you're refining an existing project or starting something new, let your imagination guide you.

Affirmation & Gratitude

I trust in my creativity to bring new and exciting opportunities into my life.

Cancer

26 May 2025

Dear Cancerian, relationships are highlighted today, with opportunities to deepen emotional bonds with loved ones. Meaningful conversations will enhance your connections. Be open, kind, and empathetic in your interactions.

Affirmation & Gratitude

I nurture my relationships with love, honesty, and empathy, fostering deeper emotional bonds with those I care about.

Cancer

27 May 2025

Dear Cancerian, career growth is in the spotlight today. The energy supports taking bold steps toward your professional goals. Stay proactive and confident in your abilities as you pursue your aspirations.

Affirmation & Gratitude

I trust in my hard work and dedication to lead me toward career success and personal growth.

Cancer

28 May 2025

Dear Cancerian, financial clarity is key today. Reassessing your financial goals and ensuring your decisions align with them will bring peace of mind. Practical planning today will secure your future.

Affirmation & Gratitude

I make responsible financial decisions that ensure stability and peace in my life.

Cancer

29 May 2025

Dear Cancerian, creativity is heightened today, offering a great opportunity to explore new artistic projects or refine ongoing ones. Let your imagination flow freely, and enjoy the creative process.

Affirmation & Gratitude

I embrace creativity in all its forms, knowing it enriches my life with joy and fulfillment.

Cancer

30 May 2025

Dear Cancerian, relationships take focus today. The cosmos encourages you to nurture your emotional connections with loved ones through open communication. Be kind, empathetic, and willing to listen, as today's energy favors deepening your bonds.

Affirmation & Gratitude

I nurture my relationships with love, honesty, and gratitude, creating deeper emotional connections with those I care about.

Cancer

31 May 2025

Dear Cancerian, career progress is in the spotlight today. The energy supports taking bold, decisive steps toward your professional aspirations. Stay confident, proactive, and focused on your long-term vision.

Affirmation & Gratitude

I trust in my hard work and skills to lead me toward career success and fulfillment.

June

2025

Cancer

1 June 2025

Dear Cancerian, today's energy supports self-care and emotional balance. Take time to reflect on your inner needs and address any areas where you may feel drained. Nurturing your emotional well-being will help restore harmony in your life. Engage in activities that bring you peace and relaxation, whether it's meditation, journaling, or connecting with loved ones.

Affirmation & Gratitude

I honor my emotional well-being, knowing that self-care brings peace and balance into my life.

Cancer

2 June 2025

Dear Cancerian, relationships are highlighted today. The cosmos encourages meaningful conversations with loved ones. Whether it's resolving misunderstandings or deepening your emotional bonds, today's energy favors openness and empathy. Be present and listen to the needs of others.

Affirmation & Gratitude

I nurture my relationships with love, honesty, and empathy, creating deeper emotional connections with those I care about.

Cancer

3 June 2025

Dear Cancerian, career growth is in focus today. The energy supports taking bold steps toward your professional goals. Whether you're expanding your role or exploring new opportunities, today's energy favors proactive action. Stay confident and trust in your abilities.

Affirmation & Gratitude

I trust in my hard work and dedication to lead me toward career success and fulfillment.

Cancer

4 June 2025

Dear Cancerian, financial decisions take priority today. Reassessing your budget and long-term goals will bring clarity and peace of mind. Thoughtful planning now will ensure stability and security in the future. Make practical choices that align with your aspirations.

Affirmation & Gratitude

I make responsible financial decisions that ensure peace, stability, and security for my future.

Cancer

5 June 2025

Dear Cancerian, creativity is heightened today. It's a perfect time to explore new artistic projects or hobbies. Let your imagination guide you, and don't be afraid to try something new. Creative expression will bring joy and fulfillment.

Affirmation & Gratitude

I embrace creativity in all its forms, knowing it brings joy and new opportunities into my life.

Cancer

6 June 2025

Dear Cancerian, relationships take focus today. The cosmos encourages deepening emotional connections with loved ones through open, honest conversations. Today's energy supports meaningful dialogue that strengthens your bonds. Be kind, empathetic, and willing to listen.

Affirmation & Gratitude

I nurture my relationships with love, empathy, and gratitude, creating deeper emotional connections with those I cherish.

Cancer

7 June 2025

Dear Cancerian, career progress is highlighted today. The energy supports making bold, proactive moves toward your professional goals. Whether you're seeking new responsibilities or expanding your role, stay focused on your long-term aspirations.

Affirmation & Gratitude

I trust in my hard work and skills to guide me toward career success and fulfillment.

Cancer

8 June 2025

Dear Cancerian, financial clarity is important today. Reassessing your budget and financial strategies will help ensure long-term stability. Today's energy favors practical decisions that bring peace of mind for your future.

Affirmation & Gratitude

I make responsible financial decisions that ensure peace, stability, and security for my future.

Cancer

9 June 2025

Dear Cancerian, creativity flows effortlessly today, offering a perfect opportunity to dive into new artistic ideas or refine ongoing projects. Let your imagination guide you toward fulfilling outcomes. Creative expression will bring joy and personal satisfaction.

Affirmation & Gratitude

I trust in my creativity to bring joy and new opportunities into my life.

Cancer

10 June 2025

Dear Cancerian, relationships are highlighted today, and the cosmos encourages nurturing your emotional connections with loved ones. Meaningful conversations will deepen your bonds and strengthen your emotional ties. Be empathetic, kind, and open to understanding others.

Affirmation & Gratitude

I nurture my relationships with love, honesty, and empathy, fostering deeper emotional bonds with those I care about.

Cancer

11 June 2025

Dear Cancerian, career growth is highlighted today. The energy supports making bold moves toward your professional goals. Whether you're seeking new opportunities or expanding your current role, stay proactive and confident in your abilities.

Affirmation & Gratitude

I trust in my hard work and dedication to guide me toward career success.

Cancer

12 June 2025

Dear Cancerian, financial planning takes center stage today. Reassessing your budget and long-term goals will bring clarity and peace of mind. Practical decisions made today will ensure stability and security for your future.

Affirmation & Gratitude

I make responsible financial decisions that bring peace, stability, and security into my life.

Cancer

13 June 2025

Dear Cancerian, creativity flows effortlessly today. Whether you're exploring new artistic ideas or refining an ongoing project, today's energy supports bold thinking and imagination. Let your creativity shine.

Affirmation & Gratitude

I embrace creativity in all its forms, knowing it enriches my life with joy and fulfillment.

Cancer

14 June 2025

Dear Cancerian, relationships take focus today. The cosmos encourages deepening emotional connections with loved ones through open, honest conversations. Be kind, empathetic, and willing to listen, as today's energy supports strengthening your bonds.

Affirmation & Gratitude

I nurture my relationships with love, honesty, and gratitude, creating deeper emotional connections with those I cherish.

Cancer

15 June 2025

Dear Cancerian, career progress is highlighted today. The energy favors making bold, proactive steps toward your professional aspirations. Whether you're expanding your responsibilities or exploring new roles, stay grounded and confident in your abilities.

Affirmation & Gratitude

I trust in my skills and hard work to guide me toward career success and personal growth.

Cancer

16 June 2025

Dear Cancerian, financial decisions are key today. Reassessing your financial goals and making thoughtful choices will ensure long-term stability. Take time to reflect on your budget and ensure it aligns with your future aspirations.

Affirmation & Gratitude

I make responsible financial decisions that bring stability and peace to my future.

Cancer

17 June 2025

Dear Cancerian, creativity is heightened today, offering a great opportunity to explore new artistic projects or refine ongoing ideas. Let your imagination guide you toward exciting possibilities. Creative expression will bring joy and fulfillment.

Affirmation & Gratitude

I trust in my creativity to open doors to new opportunities and fulfilling experiences.

Cancer

18 June 2025

Dear Cancerian, relationships are highlighted today. Focus on building deeper emotional connections with loved ones through honest and open communication. Meaningful conversations will strengthen your bonds.

Affirmation & Gratitude

I nurture my relationships with love, empathy, and kindness, fostering deeper emotional connections.

Cancer

19 June 2025

Dear Cancerian, career growth is in focus today. The cosmos supports taking bold steps toward your professional goals. Stay motivated and confident as you pursue new challenges and opportunities.

Affirmation & Gratitude

I trust in my dedication and skills to guide me toward career success.

Cancer

20 June 2025

Dear Cancerian, financial planning takes priority today. Reassessing your budget and aligning your goals with your long-term vision will bring clarity. Practical decisions today will ensure future stability and security.

Affirmation & Gratitude

I make thoughtful financial decisions that ensure peace, stability, and security for my future.

Cancer

21 June 2025

Dear Cancerian, creativity flows effortlessly today, offering a perfect opportunity to explore new artistic projects or hobbies. Let your imagination guide you toward new and exciting possibilities.

Affirmation & Gratitude

I embrace creativity in all its forms, knowing it brings joy and fulfillment into my life.

Cancer

22 June 2025

Dear Cancerian, relationships take focus today. The cosmos encourages nurturing emotional bonds with loved ones through open and honest communication. Be empathetic and willing to listen, as today's energy favors deepening your connections.

Affirmation & Gratitude

I nurture my relationships with love, honesty, and empathy, creating deeper emotional connections with those I care about.

Cancer

23 June 2025

Dear Cancerian, career progress is highlighted today. The energy supports taking proactive steps toward your professional goals. Stay confident, motivated, and focused on your long-term aspirations.

Affirmation & Gratitude

I trust in my hard work and dedication to guide me toward success and personal growth.

Cancer

24 June 2025

Dear Cancerian, financial clarity is key today. Reassessing your financial strategies and ensuring they align with your long-term goals will bring peace of mind. Practical choices made today will benefit your future.

Affirmation & Gratitude

I make responsible financial decisions that ensure stability and peace in my life.

Cancer

25 June 2025

Dear Cancerian, creativity is heightened today, making it a great time to explore new artistic ideas or refine ongoing projects. Let your imagination guide you and embrace the creative process.

Affirmation & Gratitude

I trust in my creativity to bring new and exciting opportunities into my life.

Cancer

26 June 2025

Dear Cancerian, relationships are highlighted today, with opportunities to deepen emotional bonds with loved ones. Meaningful conversations and shared experiences will strengthen your connections.

Affirmation & Gratitude

I nurture my relationships with love, empathy, and gratitude, creating deeper emotional bonds with those I cherish.

Cancer

27 June 2025

Dear Cancerian, career growth is in the spotlight today. The energy supports making bold, proactive steps toward your professional goals. Stay focused, confident, and motivated as you pursue new opportunities.

Affirmation & Gratitude

I trust in my skills and hard work to guide me toward career success and fulfillment.

Cancer

28 June 2025

Dear Cancerian, financial clarity is important today. Reassessing your budget and aligning your financial decisions with your long-term vision will ensure stability and peace. Practical choices made today will benefit your future.

Affirmation & Gratitude

I make responsible financial decisions that ensure peace, stability, and security for my future.

Cancer

29 June 2025

Dear Cancerian, creativity is heightened today, offering a great opportunity to dive into new artistic projects or refine ongoing ideas. Let your imagination guide you toward fulfilling outcomes.

Affirmation & Gratitude

I trust in my creativity to bring new and fulfilling experiences into my life.

Cancer

30 June 2025

Dear Cancerian, relationships take focus today, with the cosmos encouraging open and honest communication with loved ones. Meaningful conversations will enhance your emotional connections and bring clarity to any misunderstandings.

Affirmation & Gratitude

I nurture my relationships with love, honesty, and empathy, fostering deeper emotional bonds.

July

2025

Cancer

1 July 2025

Dear Cancerian, today's energy supports emotional healing and balance. Take time to reflect on your feelings and address any emotional stress. Nurturing your inner peace will help you restore harmony in your life. Engage in self-care activities and spend time with loved ones who uplift you.

Affirmation & Gratitude

I honor my emotional well-being, knowing that self-care brings peace and balance to my life.

Cancer

2 July 2025

Dear Cancerian, relationships take focus today. The cosmos encourages deepening your emotional bonds with loved ones through open and meaningful conversations. Be present, empathetic, and willing to listen. Today's energy supports resolving misunderstandings and building stronger connections.

Affirmation & Gratitude

I nurture my relationships with love, honesty, and empathy, fostering deeper emotional bonds with those I cherish.

Cancer

3 July 2025

Dear Cancerian, career progress is highlighted today. The energy supports taking proactive steps toward your professional goals. Whether you're expanding your responsibilities or exploring new opportunities, stay confident in your abilities. Today's energy favors bold moves that align with your long-term vision.

Affirmation & Gratitude

I trust in my hard work and dedication to guide me toward career success and fulfillment.

Cancer

4 July 2025

Dear Cancerian, financial planning is key today. Reassessing your budget and aligning your goals with your long-term vision will bring peace of mind. Practical decisions made today will ensure future stability and security. Take time to reflect on your financial habits and make adjustments if needed.

Affirmation & Gratitude

I make responsible financial decisions that bring stability and peace to my future.

Cancer

5 July 2025

Dear Cancerian, creativity is heightened today. Whether you're exploring new artistic ideas or refining ongoing projects, today's energy supports bold thinking and imagination. Let your creativity flow and embrace the joy of expression.

Affirmation & Gratitude

I embrace creativity in all its forms, knowing it enriches my life with joy and fulfillment.

Cancer

6 July 2025

Dear Cancerian, relationships take center stage today. The cosmos encourages nurturing your emotional connections with loved ones through heartfelt conversations. Be empathetic, kind, and open in your interactions. Today's energy favors strengthening your bonds and building lasting emotional ties.

Affirmation & Gratitude

I nurture my relationships with love, honesty, and gratitude, fostering deeper emotional connections with those I care about.

Cancer

7 July 2025

Dear Cancerian, career growth is in the spotlight today. The energy supports making bold, proactive moves toward your professional goals. Whether you're seeking new opportunities or expanding your role, today's energy favors forward movement. Stay focused and confident in your abilities.

Affirmation & Gratitude

I trust in my skills and dedication to guide me toward career success and fulfillment.

Cancer

8 July 2025

Dear Cancerian, financial clarity is important today. Reassessing your financial goals and aligning your budget with your long-term vision will bring peace of mind. Today's energy supports practical planning that ensures future stability and security.

Affirmation & Gratitude

I make responsible financial decisions that ensure peace, stability, and security for my future.

Cancer

9 July 2025

Dear Cancerian, creativity flows effortlessly today, making it a perfect time to dive into new artistic projects or refine ongoing ones. Let your imagination guide you, and embrace the creative process. Creative expression will bring joy and fulfillment.

Affirmation & Gratitude

I trust in my creativity to bring new and exciting opportunities into my life.

Cancer

10 July 2025

Dear Cancerian, relationships are highlighted today. The cosmos encourages open, honest communication with loved ones to strengthen emotional bonds. Be kind, empathetic, and willing to listen, as meaningful conversations will enhance your connections.

Affirmation & Gratitude

I nurture my relationships with love, honesty, and empathy, fostering deeper emotional bonds with those I care about.

Cancer

11 July 2025

Dear Cancerian, career progress is in focus today. The energy supports making proactive moves toward your professional goals. Whether you're expanding your responsibilities or exploring new opportunities, stay focused and confident in your abilities. Today's energy favors bold action.

Affirmation & Gratitude

I trust in my hard work and dedication to guide me toward career success and fulfillment.

Cancer

12 July 2025

Dear Cancerian, financial planning is key today. Reassessing your budget and aligning your financial goals with your long-term vision will bring clarity. Practical decisions made today will ensure future stability and peace of mind.

Affirmation & Gratitude

I make responsible financial decisions that ensure stability and peace for my future.

Cancer

13 July 2025

Dear Cancerian, creativity is heightened today, offering a great opportunity to explore new artistic projects or refine ongoing ideas. Let your imagination guide you toward exciting possibilities. Creative expression will bring joy and satisfaction.

Affirmation & Gratitude

I embrace creativity in all its forms, knowing it brings joy and new opportunities into my life.

Cancer

14 July 2025

Dear Cancerian, relationships take focus today, with opportunities to deepen emotional connections through open and honest conversations. Meaningful dialogue will enhance your bonds and bring clarity to any unresolved issues. Be kind, empathetic, and present in your interactions.

Affirmation & Gratitude

I nurture my relationships with love, honesty, and empathy, creating deeper emotional connections with those I care about.

Cancer

15 July 2025

Dear Cancerian, career growth is in the spotlight today. The energy supports taking bold steps toward your professional aspirations. Whether you're seeking new challenges or expanding your current role, stay confident in your abilities. Today favors proactive action toward success.

Affirmation & Gratitude

I trust in my skills and hard work to guide me toward career success and fulfillment.

Cancer

16 July 2025

Dear Cancerian, financial clarity is important today. Reassessing your budget and making thoughtful financial decisions will help ensure long-term stability. Take time to reflect on your financial goals and make adjustments as needed.

Affirmation & Gratitude

I make responsible financial decisions that bring peace, stability, and security into my life.

Cancer

17 July 2025

Dear Cancerian, creativity flows effortlessly today, making it a perfect time to dive into artistic projects or personal hobbies. Whether you're starting something new or refining an existing project, let your imagination lead the way.

Affirmation & Gratitude

I trust in my creativity to bring new and fulfilling experiences into my life.

Cancer

18 July 2025

Dear Cancerian, relationships are highlighted today. The cosmos encourages you to nurture your emotional connections with loved ones through meaningful conversations and shared experiences. Be kind, empathetic, and open to deepening your bonds.

Affirmation & Gratitude

I nurture my relationships with love, empathy, and gratitude, creating deeper emotional connections with those I cherish.

Cancer

19 July 2025

Dear Cancerian, career advancement is possible today. The energy supports making decisive moves toward your professional goals. Stay proactive and confident as you navigate new opportunities and challenges.

Affirmation & Gratitude

I trust in my hard work and dedication to guide me toward career success and personal growth.

Cancer

20 July 2025

Dear Cancerian, financial decisions take priority today. Reassessing your long-term goals and ensuring your financial strategies align with them will bring peace of mind. Practical choices made today will ensure future stability.

Affirmation & Gratitude

I make thoughtful financial decisions that ensure stability and peace for my future.

Cancer

21 July 2025

Dear Cancerian, creativity is heightened today, making it a great time to explore new ideas or artistic projects. Whether you're refining an existing project or starting something new, let your imagination flow freely.

Affirmation & Gratitude

I embrace creativity in all its forms, knowing it enriches my life with joy and fulfillment.

Cancer

22 July 2025

Dear Cancerian, relationships take center stage today. The cosmos encourages nurturing your emotional connections with loved ones through open and heartfelt communication. Be present, empathetic, and willing to listen. Today's energy favors strengthening your bonds.

Affirmation & Gratitude

I nurture my relationships with love, honesty, and gratitude, fostering deeper emotional connections with those I care about.

Cancer

23 July 2025

Dear Cancerian, career growth is in focus today. The energy supports taking bold steps toward your professional goals. Stay proactive and confident in your abilities as you pursue new challenges and opportunities.

Affirmation & Gratitude

I trust in my skills and dedication to guide me toward career success and fulfillment.

Cancer

24 July 2025

Dear Cancerian, financial clarity is important today. Reassessing your financial goals and aligning them with your long-term vision will bring peace of mind. Practical decisions made today will benefit your future security.

Affirmation & Gratitude

I make responsible financial decisions that ensure peace, stability, and security for my future.

Cancer

25 July 2025

Dear Cancerian, creativity flows effortlessly today, offering a perfect opportunity to explore new artistic ideas or refine ongoing projects. Let your imagination guide you, and embrace the creative process fully.

Affirmation & Gratitude

I trust in my creativity to bring new and fulfilling experiences into my life.

Cancer

26 July 2025

Dear Cancerian, relationships are highlighted today, and the cosmos encourages nurturing emotional connections with loved ones through open communication. Be kind, empathetic, and willing to listen, as today's energy favors strengthening your bonds.

Affirmation & Gratitude

I nurture my relationships with love, honesty, and empathy, fostering deeper emotional connections with those I care about.

Cancer

27 July 2025

Dear Cancerian, career progress is highlighted today. The energy supports taking bold, decisive steps toward your professional aspirations. Stay confident, proactive, and focused on your long-term goals.

Affirmation & Gratitude

I trust in my hard work and skills to guide me toward career success and personal growth.

Cancer

28 July 2025

Dear Cancerian, financial clarity is key today. Reassessing your budget and making responsible financial decisions will ensure future stability. Practical planning made today will bring peace and security.

Affirmation & Gratitude

I make responsible financial decisions that ensure peace, stability, and security for my future.

Cancer

29 July 2025

Dear Cancerian, creativity is heightened today, offering a great opportunity to explore new artistic projects or refine ongoing ideas. Let your imagination lead the way and enjoy the creative process.

Affirmation & Gratitude

I trust in my creativity to bring new and fulfilling experiences into my life.

Cancer

30 July 2025

Dear Cancerian, relationships take focus today. The cosmos encourages you to nurture your emotional bonds with loved ones through meaningful conversations. Open communication will strengthen your connections and bring clarity.

Affirmation & Gratitude

I nurture my relationships with love, honesty, and empathy, fostering deeper emotional connections with those I care about.

Cancer

31 July 2025

Dear Cancerian, career growth is in the spotlight today. The energy supports making bold moves toward your professional goals. Stay proactive and confident in your abilities as you pursue new opportunities.

Affirmation & Gratitude

I trust in my hard work and dedication to guide me toward career success and fulfillment.

August
2025

Cancer

1 August 2025

Dear Cancerian, today's energy supports emotional balance and self-reflection. Take time to nurture your inner peace and restore harmony in your life. Whether through mindfulness practices, creative outlets, or spending time with loved ones, focus on activities that help you recharge emotionally.

Affirmation & Gratitude

I honor my emotional well-being, knowing that self-care brings peace and balance into my life.

Cancer

2 August 2025

Dear Cancerian, relationships take focus today. The cosmos encourages you to deepen your emotional connections with loved ones. Meaningful conversations will enhance your bonds and bring clarity to unresolved issues. Be present, empathetic, and willing to listen.

Affirmation & Gratitude

I nurture my relationships with love, honesty, and empathy, fostering deeper emotional connections with those I cherish.

Cancer

3 August 2025

Dear Cancerian, career progress is highlighted today. The energy supports making bold moves toward your professional goals. Whether you're expanding your role or exploring new opportunities, stay proactive and confident in your abilities.

Affirmation & Gratitude

I trust in my hard work and dedication to guide me toward career success and fulfillment.

Cancer

4 August 2025

Dear Cancerian, financial clarity is key today. Reassessing your budget and aligning your financial decisions with your long-term vision will bring peace of mind. Practical choices made today will ensure stability and security for your future.

Affirmation & Gratitude

I make responsible financial decisions that bring stability and peace to my future.

Cancer

5 August 2025

Dear Cancerian, creativity is heightened today, making it an ideal time to explore new artistic projects or refine ongoing ones. Let your imagination flow and embrace the joy of creative expression. Whether you're working on personal hobbies or professional endeavors, today's energy favors bold thinking.

Affirmation & Gratitude

I embrace creativity in all its forms, knowing it enriches my life with joy and fulfillment.

Cancer

6 August 2025

Dear Cancerian, relationships take center stage today, with opportunities to strengthen emotional bonds with loved ones through open and heartfelt conversations. Be present, empathetic, and willing to listen, as today's energy supports nurturing your connections.

Affirmation & Gratitude

I nurture my relationships with love, honesty, and gratitude, creating deeper emotional bonds with those I care about.

Cancer

7 August 2025

Dear Cancerian, career growth is highlighted today. The energy supports taking proactive steps toward your professional goals. Whether you're seeking new responsibilities or expanding your current role, stay focused on your long-term aspirations and trust in your abilities.

Affirmation & Gratitude

I trust in my skills and dedication to guide me toward career success and fulfillment.

Cancer

8 August 2025

Dear Cancerian, financial decisions take priority today. Reassessing your financial goals and making thoughtful choices will bring clarity and peace. Today's energy supports practical financial planning that ensures long-term stability.

Affirmation & Gratitude

I make responsible financial decisions that ensure peace, stability, and security for my future.

Cancer

9 August 2025

Dear Cancerian, creativity flows effortlessly today, offering a perfect opportunity to dive into new artistic ventures or refine ongoing projects. Let your imagination guide you, and embrace the creative process. Creative expression will bring joy and fulfillment.

Affirmation & Gratitude

I trust in my creativity to bring new and fulfilling experiences into my life.

Cancer

10 August 2025

Dear Cancerian, relationships are highlighted today. The cosmos encourages meaningful conversations with loved ones to strengthen your emotional bonds. Be kind, empathetic, and willing to listen, as today's energy favors deepening your connections.

Affirmation & Gratitude

I nurture my relationships with love, honesty, and empathy, fostering deeper emotional connections with those I care about.

Cancer

11 August 2025

Dear Cancerian, career progress is in focus today. The energy supports making bold, decisive steps toward your professional goals. Whether you're seeking new challenges or expanding your current role, stay confident and proactive in your approach.

Affirmation & Gratitude

I trust in my hard work and dedication to guide me toward career success and personal growth.

Cancer

12 August 2025

Dear Cancerian, financial clarity is important today. Reassessing your budget and ensuring your financial decisions align with your long-term vision will bring peace of mind. Practical planning today will ensure future stability.

Affirmation & Gratitude

I make thoughtful financial decisions that ensure stability and peace for my future.

Cancer

13 August 2025

Dear Cancerian, creativity flows effortlessly today, offering a great opportunity to explore new artistic projects or refine ongoing ideas. Let your imagination guide you toward exciting possibilities, and embrace the joy of creative expression.

Affirmation & Gratitude

I trust in my creativity to bring joy and fulfillment into my life.

Cancer

14 August 2025

Dear Cancerian, relationships take focus today, with opportunities to deepen emotional connections through open, honest communication. Meaningful conversations will strengthen your bonds and bring clarity to unresolved issues. Be empathetic and kind.

Affirmation & Gratitude

I nurture my relationships with love, honesty, and empathy, creating deeper emotional connections with those I care about.

Cancer

15 August 2025

Dear Cancerian, career growth is in the spotlight today. The energy supports making proactive moves toward your professional aspirations. Stay motivated and confident as you pursue new opportunities or expand your role.

Affirmation & Gratitude

I trust in my skills and hard work to guide me toward career success and fulfillment.

Cancer

16 August 2025

Dear Cancerian, financial decisions take priority today. Reassessing your financial goals and making thoughtful choices will bring clarity and ensure future stability. Focus on long-term planning and practical decisions.

Affirmation & Gratitude

I make responsible financial decisions that bring peace, stability, and security into my life.

Cancer

17 August 2025

Dear Cancerian, creativity is heightened today, making it a great time to explore new artistic projects or refine ongoing ones. Let your imagination guide you toward fulfilling outcomes. Creative expression will bring joy and satisfaction.

Affirmation & Gratitude

I embrace creativity in all its forms, knowing it enriches my life with joy and fulfillment.

Cancer

18 August 2025

Dear Cancerian, relationships take focus today. The cosmos encourages nurturing your emotional connections with loved ones through open and honest conversations. Be present and willing to listen as you strengthen your bonds.

Affirmation & Gratitude

I nurture my relationships with love, honesty, and empathy, fostering deeper emotional bonds with those I care about.

Cancer

19 August 2025

Dear Cancerian, career advancement is possible today. The energy supports making bold moves toward your professional goals. Stay proactive, confident, and motivated as you navigate new opportunities and challenges.

Affirmation & Gratitude

I trust in my hard work and dedication to guide me toward career success and personal growth.

Cancer

20 August 2025

Dear Cancerian, financial clarity is key today. Reassessing your budget and long-term goals will bring peace of mind. Practical financial decisions made today will ensure future stability. Take time to reflect on your plans.

Affirmation & Gratitude

I make thoughtful financial decisions that ensure stability and peace for my future.

Cancer

21 August 2025

Dear Cancerian, creativity flows effortlessly today, offering a perfect opportunity to explore new ideas or artistic projects. Let your imagination guide you, and enjoy the creative process fully.

Affirmation & Gratitude

I trust in my creativity to bring new and exciting experiences into my life.

Cancer

22 August 2025

Dear Cancerian, relationships are highlighted today. The cosmos encourages you to nurture your emotional connections with loved ones through open communication. Be empathetic, patient, and kind in your interactions. Today's energy favors emotional closeness.

Affirmation & Gratitude

I nurture my relationships with love, honesty, and gratitude, creating deeper emotional bonds with those I care about.

Cancer

23 August 2025

Dear Cancerian, career growth is in focus today. The energy supports taking bold, proactive steps toward your professional aspirations. Stay confident and motivated as you pursue new challenges and opportunities.

Affirmation & Gratitude

I trust in my skills and dedication to guide me toward career success and fulfillment.

Cancer

24 August 2025

Dear Cancerian, financial decisions are key today. Reassessing your long-term goals and ensuring your financial strategies align with them will bring peace of mind. Practical choices made today will benefit your future.

Affirmation & Gratitude

I make responsible financial decisions that bring stability and peace to my life.

Cancer

25 August 2025

Dear Cancerian, creativity is heightened today, making it a great time to explore new artistic projects or refine ongoing ones. Let your imagination lead you toward fulfilling outcomes. Creative expression will bring joy and fulfillment.

Affirmation & Gratitude

I trust in my creativity to bring new and fulfilling experiences into my life.

Cancer

26 August 2025

Dear Cancerian, relationships take center stage today, with the cosmos encouraging open, heartfelt conversations with loved ones. Be present, empathetic, and willing to listen. Strengthen your emotional bonds through meaningful dialogue.

Affirmation & Gratitude

I nurture my relationships with love, honesty, and empathy, creating deeper emotional connections with those I cherish.

Cancer

27 August 2025

Dear Cancerian, career progress is highlighted today. The energy supports making bold, decisive steps toward your professional goals. Stay focused and confident as you pursue new opportunities and expand your role.

Affirmation & Gratitude

I trust in my hard work and skills to guide me toward success and personal growth.

Cancer

28 August 2025

Dear Cancerian, financial clarity is important today. Reassessing your financial plans and making responsible decisions will ensure future stability. Practical choices made today will benefit your long-term security.

Affirmation & Gratitude

I make responsible financial decisions that bring peace, stability, and security into my life.

Cancer

29 August 2025

Dear Cancerian, creativity is heightened today. It's a perfect time to explore new artistic ideas or refine ongoing projects. Let your imagination guide you toward exciting possibilities, and embrace the joy of creative expression.

Affirmation & Gratitude

I trust in my creativity to bring joy and fulfillment into my life.

Cancer

30 August 2025

Dear Cancerian, relationships take focus today, with opportunities to deepen emotional bonds with loved ones through open communication. Meaningful conversations will enhance your connections and bring clarity. Be empathetic and kind.

Affirmation & Gratitude

I nurture my relationships with love, honesty, and empathy, fostering deeper emotional connections with those I care about.

Cancer

31 August 2025

Dear Cancerian, career growth is in the spotlight today. The energy supports making proactive moves toward your professional goals. Stay motivated and confident in your abilities as you pursue new challenges and opportunities.

Affirmation & Gratitude

I trust in my hard work and dedication to guide me toward career success and fulfillment.

September

2025

Cancer

1 September 2025

Dear Cancerian, today's energy supports emotional healing and balance. Take time to nurture your inner peace and reflect on your emotional needs. Focus on activities that restore your balance, such as meditation or spending time in nature. Prioritize self-care and give yourself the space to recharge.

Affirmation & Gratitude

I honor my emotional well-being, knowing that self-care brings peace and balance into my life.

Cancer

2 September 2025

Dear Cancerian, relationships take focus today. The cosmos encourages meaningful conversations with loved ones. Be present and listen to their needs. Today's energy supports open dialogue and resolving any lingering misunderstandings. Strengthening your emotional bonds will bring you closer.

Affirmation & Gratitude

I nurture my relationships with love, honesty, and empathy, creating deeper emotional connections with those I care about.

Cancer

3 September 2025

Dear Cancerian, career growth is in focus today. The energy supports making bold moves toward your professional goals. Whether you're expanding your current role or seeking new opportunities, today's energy favors taking decisive steps. Trust in your skills and stay proactive.

Affirmation & Gratitude

I trust in my hard work and dedication to guide me toward career success and fulfillment.

Cancer

4 September 2025

Dear Cancerian, financial planning is key today. Reassessing your budget and long-term financial goals will bring peace of mind. Practical choices made now will ensure stability for the future. Be mindful of your spending and align your financial decisions with your aspirations.

Affirmation & Gratitude

I make responsible financial decisions that bring peace, stability, and security for my future.

Cancer

5 September 2025

Dear Cancerian, creativity is heightened today, offering a perfect opportunity to explore new artistic projects or refine ongoing ones. Let your imagination guide you, and embrace the joy of creative expression. Whether you're working on a hobby or professional venture, today's energy favors bold thinking.

Affirmation & Gratitude

I embrace creativity in all its forms, knowing it enriches my life with joy and fulfillment.

Cancer

6 September 2025

Dear Cancerian, relationships take center stage today. The cosmos encourages nurturing your emotional connections with loved ones through open and heartfelt conversations. Be present, empathetic, and willing to listen, as today's energy supports strengthening your bonds.

Affirmation & Gratitude

I nurture my relationships with love, honesty, and gratitude, creating deeper emotional bonds with those I cherish.

Cancer

7 September 2025

Dear Cancerian, career growth is in the spotlight today. The energy supports making proactive moves toward your professional aspirations. Stay motivated and confident as you pursue new challenges and expand your role. Trust in your abilities to succeed.

Affirmation & Gratitude

I trust in my skills and hard work to guide me toward career success and fulfillment.

Cancer

8 September 2025

Dear Cancerian, financial decisions take priority today. Reassessing your financial goals and making thoughtful choices will bring clarity and security. Today's energy supports practical financial planning that ensures long-term stability.

Affirmation & Gratitude

I make responsible financial decisions that bring peace, stability, and security into my life.

Cancer

9 September 2025

Dear Cancerian, creativity flows effortlessly today, making it a perfect time to dive into artistic projects or explore new ideas. Let your imagination guide you and embrace the creative process. Creative expression will bring joy and personal satisfaction.

Affirmation & Gratitude

I trust in my creativity to bring joy and new possibilities into my life.

Cancer

10 September 2025

Dear Cancerian, relationships are highlighted today. The cosmos encourages open and honest communication with loved ones. Meaningful conversations will deepen your emotional bonds and bring clarity to unresolved issues. Be empathetic and patient.

Affirmation & Gratitude

I nurture my relationships with love, honesty, and empathy, fostering deeper emotional connections with those I care about.

Cancer

11 September 2025

Dear Cancerian, career progress is in focus today. The energy supports taking decisive steps toward your professional goals. Whether you're seeking new responsibilities or exploring new opportunities, today's energy favors bold action. Stay proactive and confident in your abilities.

Affirmation & Gratitude

I trust in my hard work and dedication to guide me toward career success and personal growth.

Cancer

12 September 2025

Dear Cancerian, financial clarity is important today. Reassessing your budget and aligning your financial decisions with your long-term goals will bring peace of mind. Practical choices made today will ensure future stability and security.

Affirmation & Gratitude

I make responsible financial decisions that ensure stability and peace for my future.

Cancer

13 September 2025

Dear Cancerian, creativity is heightened today. Whether you're exploring new artistic projects or refining ongoing ones, let your imagination guide you toward fulfilling outcomes. Creative expression will bring joy and satisfaction.

Affirmation & Gratitude

I embrace creativity in all its forms, knowing it enriches my life with joy and fulfillment.

Cancer

14 September 2025

Dear Cancerian, relationships take focus today, with the cosmos encouraging you to deepen your emotional bonds with loved ones. Open, honest communication will strengthen your connections and bring clarity to unresolved issues. Be kind, empathetic, and present.

Affirmation & Gratitude

I nurture my relationships with love, honesty, and empathy, creating deeper emotional connections with those I care about.

Cancer

15 September 2025

Dear Cancerian, career growth is highlighted today. The energy supports making bold moves toward your professional goals. Stay motivated and proactive as you navigate new challenges and opportunities. Trust in your abilities to succeed.

Affirmation & Gratitude

I trust in my skills and hard work to guide me toward career success and fulfillment.

Cancer

16 September 2025

Dear Cancerian, financial planning is key today. Reassessing your budget and ensuring your goals align with your long-term vision will bring peace of mind. Today's energy supports practical financial decisions that ensure future stability.

Affirmation & Gratitude

I make responsible financial decisions that ensure peace, stability, and security for my future.

Cancer

17 September 2025

Dear Cancerian, creativity flows effortlessly today, making it a great time to explore new artistic projects or refine ongoing ones. Let your imagination guide you toward fulfilling outcomes, and embrace the joy of creative expression.

Affirmation & Gratitude

I trust in my creativity to bring joy and new opportunities into my life.

Cancer

18 September 2025

Dear Cancerian, relationships are highlighted today, with opportunities to deepen emotional connections through meaningful conversations. Be open, honest, and willing to listen, as today's energy favors strengthening your bonds.

Affirmation & Gratitude

I nurture my relationships with love, honesty, and empathy, creating deeper emotional bonds with those I care about.

Cancer

19 September 2025

Dear Cancerian, career progress is in the spotlight today. The energy supports taking bold, decisive steps toward your professional aspirations. Stay confident and focused as you pursue new opportunities and expand your role.

Affirmation & Gratitude

I trust in my hard work and dedication to guide me toward career success and personal growth.

Cancer

20 September 2025

Dear Cancerian, financial clarity is key today. Reassessing your financial plans and making responsible decisions will ensure future stability. Practical choices made today will benefit your long-term security.

Affirmation & Gratitude

I make thoughtful financial decisions that bring peace, stability, and security to my life.

Cancer

21 September 2025

Dear Cancerian, creativity is heightened today, offering a great opportunity to explore new artistic projects or refine ongoing ideas. Let your imagination guide you toward exciting possibilities. Creative expression will bring joy and fulfillment.

Affirmation & Gratitude

I trust in my creativity to bring new and fulfilling experiences into my life.

Cancer

22 September 2025

Dear Cancerian, relationships take focus today, with opportunities to deepen emotional bonds with loved ones through open communication. Meaningful conversations will enhance your connections and bring clarity to unresolved issues. Be empathetic and kind.

Affirmation & Gratitude

I nurture my relationships with love, honesty, and empathy, fostering deeper emotional connections with those I care about.

Cancer

23 September 2025

Dear Cancerian, career growth is in focus today. The energy supports taking bold, proactive steps toward your professional goals. Stay motivated and confident as you pursue new challenges and opportunities.

Affirmation & Gratitude

I trust in my skills and dedication to guide me toward career success and fulfillment.

Cancer

24 September 2025

Dear Cancerian, financial clarity is important today. Reassessing your financial goals and aligning them with your long-term vision will bring peace of mind. Practical decisions made today will benefit your future.

Affirmation & Gratitude

I make responsible financial decisions that ensure peace, stability, and security for my future.

Cancer

25 September 2025

Dear Cancerian, creativity flows effortlessly today, making it a great time to explore new artistic ideas or refine ongoing projects. Let your imagination lead you toward exciting possibilities, and enjoy the creative process.

Affirmation & Gratitude

I trust in my creativity to bring joy and fulfillment into my life.

Cancer

26 September 2025

Dear Cancerian, relationships take focus today, with opportunities to strengthen emotional connections with loved ones. Meaningful conversations and shared experiences will enhance your bonds and bring clarity. Be kind, empathetic, and open in your interactions.

Affirmation & Gratitude

I nurture my relationships with love, honesty, and gratitude, creating deeper emotional connections with those I care about.

Cancer

27 September 2025

Dear Cancerian, career progress is in focus today. The energy supports making bold, decisive steps toward your professional goals. Stay confident and proactive as you pursue new opportunities and expand your role.

Affirmation & Gratitude

I trust in my hard work and skills to guide me toward success and fulfillment in my career.

Cancer

28 September 2025

Dear Cancerian, financial planning takes priority today. Reassessing your budget and aligning your financial decisions with your long-term vision will ensure peace of mind. Practical choices made today will benefit your future stability.

Affirmation & Gratitude

I make thoughtful financial decisions that bring stability and peace to my life.

Cancer

29 September 2025

Dear Cancerian, creativity is heightened today, making it a great time to dive into new artistic projects or refine ongoing ideas. Let your imagination guide you toward fulfilling outcomes and embrace the joy of expression.

Affirmation & Gratitude

I trust in my creativity to bring new and exciting experiences into my life.

Cancer

30 September 2025

Dear Cancerian, relationships are highlighted today, with opportunities to strengthen your emotional connections through open and honest communication. Meaningful conversations will deepen your bonds and bring clarity to any unresolved issues.

Affirmation & Gratitude

I nurture my relationships with love, honesty, and empathy, fostering deeper emotional connections with those I care about.

October

2025

Cancer

1 October 2025

Dear Cancerian, today's energy supports emotional healing and self-reflection. Take time to assess your emotional needs and address any unresolved feelings. Nurturing your inner self will bring balance and peace to your life. Engage in self-care and activities that allow you to recharge emotionally.

Affirmation & Gratitude

I honor my emotional well-being, knowing that self-care brings peace and balance to my life.

Cancer

2 October 2025

Dear Cancerian, relationships take focus today. The cosmos encourages open communication with loved ones. Meaningful conversations and shared experiences will strengthen your emotional bonds. Be empathetic, kind, and willing to listen. Strengthening your relationships will bring emotional fulfillment.

Affirmation & Gratitude

I nurture my relationships with love, honesty, and empathy, creating deeper emotional bonds with those I care about.

Cancer

3 October 2025

Dear Cancerian, career progress is highlighted today. The energy supports taking decisive steps toward your professional goals. Stay proactive, confident, and focused on your long-term aspirations as you pursue new opportunities and challenges.

Affirmation & Gratitude

I trust in my hard work and dedication to guide me toward career success and fulfillment.

Cancer

4 October 2025

Dear Cancerian, financial clarity is important today. Reassessing your financial plans and ensuring they align with your long-term goals will bring peace of mind. Practical decisions made today will benefit your future stability.

Affirmation & Gratitude

I make responsible financial decisions that ensure peace, stability, and security for my future.

Cancer

5 October 2025

Dear Cancerian, creativity is heightened today. Whether you're working on new artistic projects or refining ongoing ones, today's energy supports bold thinking and imagination. Let your creativity guide you and embrace the joy of expression.

Affirmation & Gratitude

I embrace creativity in all its forms, knowing it enriches my life with joy and fulfillment.

Cancer

6 October 2025

Dear Cancerian, relationships take center stage today. The cosmos encourages deepening emotional connections with loved ones through open and meaningful conversations. Be present, empathetic, and willing to listen. Strengthening your bonds will bring emotional closeness.

Affirmation & Gratitude

I nurture my relationships with love, honesty, and gratitude, creating deeper emotional bonds with those I care about.

Cancer

7 October 2025

Dear Cancerian, career growth is highlighted today. The energy supports making bold moves toward your professional aspirations. Stay confident and proactive as you navigate new challenges and pursue new opportunities. Trust in your skills and remain focused.

Affirmation & Gratitude

I trust in my hard work and skills to guide me toward career success and fulfillment.

Cancer

8 October 2025

Dear Cancerian, financial decisions take priority today. Reassessing your budget and aligning your financial choices with your long-term goals will bring clarity and peace of mind. Practical planning today will ensure future stability.

Affirmation & Gratitude

I make thoughtful financial decisions that bring peace, stability, and security to my life.

Cancer

9 October 2025

Dear Cancerian, creativity flows effortlessly today, making it a perfect time to dive into artistic projects or explore new ideas. Let your imagination guide you toward fulfilling outcomes. Creative expression will bring joy and satisfaction.

Affirmation & Gratitude

I trust in my creativity to bring joy and new possibilities into my life.

Cancer

10 October 2025

Dear Cancerian, relationships are highlighted today. The cosmos encourages open, honest communication with loved ones. Meaningful conversations will strengthen your emotional bonds and bring clarity to unresolved issues. Be kind and empathetic in your interactions.

Affirmation & Gratitude

I nurture my relationships with love, honesty, and empathy, fostering deeper emotional connections with those I care about.

Cancer

11 October 2025

Dear Cancerian, career progress is in focus today. The energy supports making bold moves toward your professional goals. Stay proactive and confident as you take on new challenges. Trust in your abilities and maintain your long-term vision.

Affirmation & Gratitude

I trust in my hard work and dedication to guide me toward career success and fulfillment.

Cancer

12 October 2025

Dear Cancerian, financial clarity is important today. Reassessing your financial goals and aligning your budget with your long-term vision will bring peace of mind. Practical decisions made today will ensure future stability.

Affirmation & Gratitude

I make responsible financial decisions that bring peace, stability, and security to my future.

Cancer

13 October 2025

Dear Cancerian, creativity is heightened today, offering a perfect opportunity to explore new artistic projects or refine ongoing ideas. Let your imagination guide you and embrace the joy of creative expression.

Affirmation & Gratitude

I trust in my creativity to bring joy and new opportunities into my life.

Cancer

14 October 2025

Dear Cancerian, relationships take focus today. The cosmos encourages meaningful conversations with loved ones to deepen your emotional connections. Be present, empathetic, and willing to listen, as today's energy favors emotional closeness and mutual understanding.

Affirmation & Gratitude

I nurture my relationships with love, honesty, and empathy, creating deeper emotional bonds with those I care about.

Cancer

15 October 2025

Dear Cancerian, career growth is highlighted today. The energy supports making decisive moves toward your professional goals. Stay confident and proactive as you pursue new challenges and opportunities. Trust in your skills and hard work to guide you forward.

Affirmation & Gratitude

I trust in my skills and dedication to guide me toward career success and personal growth.

Cancer

16 October 2025

Dear Cancerian, financial decisions take priority today. Reassessing your budget and aligning your financial strategies with your long-term goals will bring clarity and peace of mind. Practical planning today will ensure future security.

Affirmation & Gratitude

I make responsible financial decisions that bring stability and peace into my life.

Cancer

17 October 2025

Dear Cancerian, creativity flows effortlessly today, making it a great time to dive into artistic projects or explore new ideas. Let your imagination guide you, and enjoy the creative process. Creative expression will bring fulfillment and joy.

Affirmation & Gratitude

I trust in my creativity to bring joy and new experiences into my life.

Cancer

18 October 2025

Dear Cancerian, relationships take center stage today. The cosmos encourages nurturing your emotional connections with loved ones through open and honest communication. Be kind, empathetic, and present, as today's energy supports deepening your bonds.

Affirmation & Gratitude

I nurture my relationships with love, honesty, and gratitude, fostering deeper emotional connections with those I cherish.

Cancer

19 October 2025

Dear Cancerian, career progress is highlighted today. The energy supports making bold, decisive moves toward your professional aspirations. Stay focused, proactive, and confident in your abilities as you pursue new opportunities.

Affirmation & Gratitude

I trust in my hard work and dedication to guide me toward career success and personal fulfillment.

Cancer

20 October 2025

Dear Cancerian, financial clarity is key today. Reassessing your long-term goals and ensuring your financial plans align with them will bring peace of mind. Practical choices made today will secure future stability.

Affirmation & Gratitude

I make thoughtful financial decisions that ensure peace, stability, and security for my future.

Cancer

21 October 2025

Dear Cancerian, creativity is heightened today, offering a great opportunity to explore new artistic ventures or refine ongoing projects. Let your imagination lead the way, and embrace the joy of creative expression.

Affirmation & Gratitude

I embrace creativity in all its forms, knowing it brings fulfillment and joy to my life.

Cancer

22 October 2025

Dear Cancerian, relationships are in focus today, and the cosmos encourages you to nurture emotional bonds with loved ones. Meaningful conversations and shared experiences will deepen your connections and strengthen your relationships. Be kind and empathetic.

Affirmation & Gratitude

I nurture my relationships with love, honesty, and empathy, creating deeper emotional connections with those I care about.

Cancer

23 October 2025

Dear Cancerian, career growth is in the spotlight today. The energy supports making proactive moves toward your professional goals. Stay motivated, confident, and focused on long-term success as you navigate new challenges.

Affirmation & Gratitude

I trust in my skills and hard work to guide me toward career success and fulfillment.

Cancer

24 October 2025

Dear Cancerian, financial planning is key today. Reassessing your budget and aligning your financial goals with your long-term vision will bring peace of mind. Practical choices made today will benefit your future stability.

Affirmation & Gratitude

I make responsible financial decisions that ensure stability and peace for my future.

Cancer

25 October 2025

Dear Cancerian, creativity flows effortlessly today, making it a great time to explore new artistic ideas or refine ongoing projects. Let your imagination guide you, and embrace the joy of creative expression.

Affirmation & Gratitude

I trust in my creativity to bring joy and fulfillment into my life.

Cancer

26 October 2025

Dear Cancerian, relationships take focus today, with opportunities to strengthen your emotional bonds through open and honest communication. Meaningful conversations will enhance your connections and bring clarity to unresolved issues.

Affirmation & Gratitude

I nurture my relationships with love, honesty, and empathy, fostering deeper emotional bonds with those I care about.

Cancer

27 October 2025

Dear Cancerian, career progress is highlighted today. The energy supports taking bold, decisive steps toward your professional goals. Stay proactive and confident in your abilities as you pursue new opportunities and expand your role.

Affirmation & Gratitude

I trust in my hard work and skills to guide me toward success and fulfillment in my career.

Cancer

28 October 2025

Dear Cancerian, financial clarity is important today. Reassessing your budget and ensuring your financial plans align with your long-term goals will bring peace of mind. Practical decisions made today will benefit your future.

Affirmation & Gratitude

I make responsible financial decisions that bring peace, stability, and security into my life.

Cancer

29 October 2025

Dear Cancerian, creativity is heightened today, making it a perfect time to dive into new artistic projects or refine ongoing ideas. Let your imagination guide you toward fulfilling outcomes, and embrace the joy of creative expression.

Affirmation & Gratitude

I trust in my creativity to bring new and fulfilling experiences into my life.

Cancer

30 October 2025

Dear Cancerian, relationships are highlighted today. The cosmos encourages you to nurture emotional bonds with loved ones through open, meaningful conversations. Be present, kind, and empathetic, as today's energy favors emotional closeness and clarity.

Affirmation & Gratitude

I nurture my relationships with love, honesty, and empathy, fostering deeper emotional connections with those I care about.

Cancer

31 October 2025

Dear Cancerian, career growth is in the spotlight today. The energy supports making proactive moves toward your professional goals. Stay confident, motivated, and focused on long-term success as you pursue new challenges.

Affirmation & Gratitude

I trust in my hard work and dedication to guide me toward career success and fulfillment

November

2025

Cancer

1 November 2025

Dear Cancerian, today's energy supports emotional healing and reflection. Take time to focus on your inner self, and address any lingering feelings. Nurturing your emotional well-being will restore balance and peace to your life. Self-care activities and mindfulness will help you recharge.

Affirmation & Gratitude

I honor my emotional well-being, knowing that self-care brings peace and balance into my life.

Cancer

2 November 2025

Dear Cancerian, relationships take focus today. The cosmos encourages you to connect with loved ones through meaningful conversations. Be present, empathetic, and willing to listen. Strengthening your emotional bonds will bring you closer to those you care about.

Affirmation & Gratitude

I nurture my relationships with love, honesty, and empathy, creating deeper emotional connections with those I cherish.

Cancer

3 November 2025

Dear Cancerian, career growth is in focus today. The energy supports making bold, decisive steps toward your professional goals. Whether you're expanding your role or seeking new opportunities, today's energy favors forward movement. Stay proactive and confident in your abilities.

Affirmation & Gratitude

I trust in my hard work and dedication to guide me toward career success and fulfillment.

Cancer

4 November 2025

Dear Cancerian, financial planning is key today. Reassessing your budget and long-term goals will bring clarity and peace of mind. Practical decisions made now will ensure future stability and security. Align your financial habits with your aspirations for a stable future.

Affirmation & Gratitude

I make responsible financial decisions that ensure peace, stability, and security for my future.

Cancer

5 November 2025

Dear Cancerian, creativity flows effortlessly today, offering a great opportunity to dive into artistic projects or explore new ideas. Let your imagination guide you, and embrace the creative process. Creative expression will bring joy and personal satisfaction.

Affirmation & Gratitude

I trust in my creativity to bring joy and new possibilities into my life.

Cancer

6 November 2025

Dear Cancerian, relationships take center stage today. The cosmos encourages you to nurture your emotional connections with loved ones through open, honest conversations. Be kind, empathetic, and present, as today's energy supports deepening your bonds.

Affirmation & Gratitude

I nurture my relationships with love, honesty, and gratitude, creating deeper emotional bonds with those I care about.

Cancer

7 November 2025

Dear Cancerian, career progress is highlighted today. The energy supports making proactive moves toward your professional goals. Stay motivated and confident as you navigate new challenges. Trust in your skills to guide you forward.

Affirmation & Gratitude

I trust in my hard work and skills to lead me toward career success and personal growth.

Cancer

8 November 2025

Dear Cancerian, financial decisions take priority today. Reassessing your financial plans and making thoughtful choices will bring clarity and ensure future stability. Practical decisions made today will align with your long-term aspirations.

Affirmation & Gratitude

I make thoughtful financial decisions that bring peace, stability, and security to my future.

Cancer

9 November 2025

Dear Cancerian, creativity is heightened today. Whether you're exploring new artistic ideas or refining an ongoing project, let your imagination lead you. Embrace bold thinking and the joy of creative expression.

Affirmation & Gratitude

I embrace creativity in all its forms, knowing it brings joy and fulfillment to my life.

Cancer

10 November 2025

Dear Cancerian, relationships take focus today. The cosmos encourages meaningful conversations with loved ones to deepen emotional connections. Be empathetic, kind, and willing to listen, as today's energy favors strengthening bonds.

Affirmation & Gratitude

I nurture my relationships with love, honesty, and empathy, fostering deeper emotional connections with those I cherish.

Cancer

11 November 2025

Dear Cancerian, career growth is highlighted today. The energy supports making bold moves toward your professional goals. Stay proactive and confident as you pursue new challenges and opportunities. Trust in your abilities to succeed.

Affirmation & Gratitude

I trust in my skills and dedication to guide me toward career success and fulfillment.

Cancer

12 November 2025

Dear Cancerian, financial clarity is important today. Reassessing your budget and aligning your financial goals with your long-term vision will bring peace of mind. Practical decisions made today will ensure future stability.

Affirmation & Gratitude

I make responsible financial decisions that ensure peace, stability, and security for my future.

Cancer

13 November 2025

Dear Cancerian, creativity flows effortlessly today, making it a perfect time to explore new artistic projects or refine ongoing ideas. Let your imagination guide you toward exciting possibilities. Creative expression will bring joy and satisfaction.

Affirmation & Gratitude

I trust in my creativity to bring joy and new opportunities into my life.

Cancer

14 November 2025

Dear Cancerian, relationships take focus today, with opportunities to deepen emotional bonds through open and honest communication. Meaningful conversations will strengthen your connections and bring clarity. Be empathetic, kind, and willing to listen.

Affirmation & Gratitude

I nurture my relationships with love, honesty, and empathy, creating deeper emotional bonds with those I care about.

Cancer

15 November 2025

Dear Cancerian, career growth is in the spotlight today. The energy supports taking proactive steps toward your professional goals. Stay focused and confident as you navigate new opportunities and expand your role.

Affirmation & Gratitude

I trust in my hard work and dedication to guide me toward career success and personal growth.

Cancer

16 November 2025

Dear Cancerian, financial decisions take priority today. Reassessing your long-term goals and ensuring your financial strategies align with them will bring peace of mind. Practical choices made today will benefit your future.

Affirmation & Gratitude

I make thoughtful financial decisions that ensure stability and peace for my future.

Cancer

17 November 2025

Dear Cancerian, creativity is heightened today, making it a great time to dive into new artistic projects or refine ongoing ideas. Let your imagination guide you, and enjoy the creative process.

Affirmation & Gratitude

I trust in my creativity to bring new and fulfilling experiences into my life.

Cancer

18 November 2025

Dear Cancerian, relationships take center stage today. The cosmos encourages nurturing emotional connections with loved ones through open communication. Be kind, empathetic, and present as you strengthen your bonds.

Affirmation & Gratitude

I nurture my relationships with love, honesty, and gratitude, creating deeper emotional connections with those I cherish.

Cancer

19 November 2025

Dear Cancerian, career progress is highlighted today. The energy supports making bold, decisive steps toward your professional goals. Stay proactive and confident in your abilities as you pursue new challenges.

Affirmation & Gratitude

I trust in my hard work and skills to guide me toward success and fulfillment in my career.

Cancer

20 November 2025

Dear Cancerian, financial clarity is key today. Reassessing your budget and aligning your financial plans with your long-term goals will bring peace of mind. Practical decisions made today will benefit your future.

Affirmation & Gratitude

I make responsible financial decisions that ensure peace, stability, and security for my future.

Cancer

21 November 2025

Dear Cancerian, creativity is heightened today, making it a perfect time to explore new artistic projects or refine ongoing ideas. Let your imagination guide you toward fulfilling outcomes, and embrace the joy of creative expression.

Affirmation & Gratitude

I trust in my creativity to bring joy and fulfillment into my life.

Cancer

22 November 2025

Dear Cancerian, relationships take focus today, with opportunities to strengthen emotional connections with loved ones through open and honest communication. Meaningful conversations will deepen your bonds and bring clarity.

Affirmation & Gratitude

I nurture my relationships with love, honesty, and empathy, fostering deeper emotional connections with those I care about.

Cancer

23 November 2025

Dear Cancerian, career growth is in the spotlight today. The energy supports taking bold, proactive steps toward your professional goals. Stay motivated and confident as you pursue new challenges and expand your role.

Affirmation & Gratitude

I trust in my skills and hard work to guide me toward career success and fulfillment.

Cancer

24 November 2025

Dear Cancerian, financial clarity is important today. Reassessing your budget and aligning your financial plans with your long-term goals will bring peace of mind. Practical decisions made today will benefit your future stability.

Affirmation & Gratitude

I make responsible financial decisions that ensure stability and peace for my future.

Cancer

25 November 2025

Dear Cancerian, creativity flows effortlessly today, offering a great opportunity to explore new artistic ideas or refine ongoing projects. Let your imagination guide you, and enjoy the creative process.

Affirmation & Gratitude

I trust in my creativity to bring joy and fulfillment into my life.

Cancer

26 November 2025

Dear Cancerian, relationships take focus today, with opportunities to strengthen emotional bonds through meaningful conversations. Open, honest dialogue will enhance your connections and bring clarity to unresolved issues.

Affirmation & Gratitude

I nurture my relationships with love, honesty, and empathy, fostering deeper emotional bonds with those I care about.

Cancer

27 November 2025

Dear Cancerian, career progress is highlighted today. The energy supports making bold, decisive steps toward your professional goals. Stay proactive and confident as you pursue new opportunities and expand your role.

Affirmation & Gratitude

I trust in my hard work and skills to guide me toward success and fulfillment in my career.

Cancer

28 November 2025

Dear Cancerian, financial clarity is key today. Reassessing your long-term goals and aligning your financial decisions with them will bring peace of mind. Practical choices made today will secure future stability.

Affirmation & Gratitude

I make responsible financial decisions that ensure stability and peace for my future.

Cancer

29 November 2025

Dear Cancerian, creativity is heightened today, offering a great opportunity to explore new artistic projects or refine ongoing ideas. Let your imagination guide you toward fulfilling outcomes. Creative expression will bring joy and fulfillment.

Affirmation & Gratitude

I trust in my creativity to bring new and fulfilling experiences into my life.

Cancer

30 November 2025

Dear Cancerian, relationships are highlighted today, with opportunities to deepen emotional bonds through open, meaningful communication. Meaningful conversations will enhance your connections and bring clarity. Be empathetic and kind.

Affirmation & Gratitude

I nurture my relationships with love, honesty, and empathy, fostering deeper emotional bonds with those I care about.

December

2025

Cancer

1 December 2025

Dear Cancerian, today's energy supports emotional healing and balance. Take time to reflect on your personal growth and emotional needs. Self-care and mindfulness will help restore inner peace and harmony.

Affirmation & Gratitude

I honor my emotional well-being, knowing that self-care brings peace and balance into my life.

Cancer

2 December 2025

Dear Cancerian, relationships take focus today. The cosmos encourages you to nurture your emotional bonds with loved ones through open and meaningful conversations. Be kind, empathetic, and willing to listen. Strengthening your relationships will bring emotional fulfillment.

Affirmation & Gratitude

I nurture my relationships with love, honesty, and empathy, fostering deeper emotional connections with those I care about.

Cancer

3 December 2025

Dear Cancerian, career growth is highlighted today. The energy supports making bold moves toward your professional goals. Stay proactive and confident as you pursue new challenges. Trust in your abilities to succeed.

Affirmation & Gratitude

I trust in my hard work and dedication to guide me toward career success and fulfillment.

Cancer

4 December 2025

Dear Cancerian, financial clarity is important today. Reassessing your budget and ensuring your financial decisions align with your long-term goals will bring peace of mind. Practical decisions made today will ensure future stability.

Affirmation & Gratitude

I make responsible financial decisions that ensure peace, stability, and security for my future.

Cancer

5 December 2025

Dear Cancerian, creativity flows effortlessly today, offering a great opportunity to explore new artistic projects or refine ongoing ones. Let your imagination guide you, and embrace the creative process. Creative expression will bring joy and fulfillment.

Affirmation & Gratitude

I trust in my creativity to bring joy and new possibilities into my life.

Cancer

6 December 2025

Dear Cancerian, relationships take center stage today. The cosmos encourages nurturing your emotional connections with loved ones through open, honest conversations. Be present and empathetic as you strengthen your bonds.

Affirmation & Gratitude

I nurture my relationships with love, honesty, and gratitude, creating deeper emotional bonds with those I cherish.

Cancer

7 December 2025

Dear Cancerian, career progress is in focus today. The energy supports making bold, proactive moves toward your professional goals. Stay motivated and confident as you pursue new challenges and opportunities. Trust in your skills and dedication to guide you forward.

Affirmation & Gratitude

I trust in my hard work and skills to lead me toward career success and personal growth.

Cancer

8 December 2025

Dear Cancerian, financial decisions take priority today. Reassessing your long-term financial goals and ensuring they align with your future vision will bring clarity and security. Practical decisions made today will ensure future stability.

Affirmation & Gratitude

I make thoughtful financial decisions that bring peace, stability, and security to my future.

Cancer

9 December 2025

Dear Cancerian, creativity is heightened today. Whether you're exploring new artistic ideas or refining ongoing projects, today's energy supports bold thinking and imagination. Let your creativity flow freely.

Affirmation & Gratitude

I embrace creativity in all its forms, knowing it enriches my life with joy and fulfillment.

Cancer

10 December 2025

Dear Cancerian, relationships take focus today. The cosmos encourages deepening emotional connections with loved ones through meaningful conversations. Be kind, empathetic, and present, as today's energy supports nurturing your bonds.

Affirmation & Gratitude

I nurture my relationships with love, honesty, and empathy, creating deeper emotional connections with those I care about.

Cancer

11 December 2025

Dear Cancerian, career growth is highlighted today. The energy supports taking decisive steps toward your professional goals. Stay proactive and confident as you pursue new challenges. Trust in your abilities to achieve success.

Affirmation & Gratitude

I trust in my hard work and dedication to guide me toward career success and fulfillment.

Cancer

12 December 2025

Dear Cancerian, financial clarity is important today. Reassessing your long-term goals and making practical decisions will ensure stability and security. Today's energy supports thoughtful financial planning.

Affirmation & Gratitude

I make responsible financial decisions that bring peace, stability, and security into my life.

Cancer

13 December 2025

Dear Cancerian, creativity flows effortlessly today, offering a great opportunity to explore new artistic projects or refine ongoing ones. Let your imagination guide you, and embrace the joy of creative expression.

Affirmation & Gratitude

I trust in my creativity to bring new and fulfilling experiences into my life.

Cancer

14 December 2025

Dear Cancerian, relationships take focus today. The cosmos encourages nurturing emotional connections with loved ones through open and honest communication. Be present and empathetic, as today's energy favors deepening your bonds.

Affirmation & Gratitude

I nurture my relationships with love, honesty, and empathy, creating deeper emotional bonds with those I care about.

Cancer

15 December 2025

Dear Cancerian, career progress is in the spotlight today. The energy supports taking bold, proactive steps toward your professional goals. Stay confident and focused on your long-term aspirations as you pursue new opportunities.

Affirmation & Gratitude

I trust in my hard work and skills to guide me toward career success and personal growth.

Cancer

16 December 2025

Dear Cancerian, financial decisions take priority today. Reassessing your budget and aligning your financial goals with your long-term vision will bring peace of mind. Practical decisions made today will ensure future stability.

Affirmation & Gratitude

I make thoughtful financial decisions that bring stability and peace to my future.

Cancer

17 December 2025

Dear Cancerian, creativity is heightened today, making it a perfect time to explore new artistic ideas or refine ongoing projects. Let your imagination guide you, and embrace the joy of creative expression.

Affirmation & Gratitude

I trust in my creativity to bring joy and fulfillment into my life.

Cancer

18 December 2025

Dear Cancerian, relationships take center stage today. The cosmos encourages nurturing your emotional connections with loved ones through meaningful conversations. Be kind, empathetic, and willing to listen. Strengthening your bonds will bring emotional closeness.

Affirmation & Gratitude

I nurture my relationships with love, honesty, and empathy, creating deeper emotional connections with those I cherish.

Cancer

19 December 2025

Dear Cancerian, career growth is in focus today. The energy supports taking bold moves toward your professional goals. Stay motivated and confident as you pursue new challenges and expand your role.

Affirmation & Gratitude

I trust in my hard work and skills to lead me toward career success and personal growth.

Cancer

20 December 2025

Dear Cancerian, financial clarity is important today. Reassessing your long-term financial goals and aligning your decisions with them will bring peace of mind. Practical choices made today will benefit your future security.

Affirmation & Gratitude

I make responsible financial decisions that ensure peace, stability, and security for my future.

Cancer

21 December 2025

Dear Cancerian, creativity is heightened today, offering a great opportunity to explore new artistic ideas or refine ongoing projects. Let your imagination guide you, and embrace the creative process.

Affirmation & Gratitude

I trust in my creativity to bring joy and new experiences into my life.

Cancer

22 December 2025

Dear Cancerian, relationships take focus today, with opportunities to deepen emotional connections with loved ones through open and honest communication. Meaningful conversations will enhance your bonds and bring clarity.

Affirmation & Gratitude

I nurture my relationships with love, honesty, and empathy, fostering deeper emotional bonds with those I care about.

Cancer

23 December 2025

Dear Cancerian, career growth is in the spotlight today. The energy supports making bold moves toward your professional aspirations. Stay proactive and confident in your abilities as you pursue new opportunities and challenges.

Affirmation & Gratitude

I trust in my skills and hard work to guide me toward career success and fulfillment.

Cancer

24 December 2025

Dear Cancerian, financial decisions are key today. Reassessing your budget and long-term financial goals will bring clarity. Practical decisions made today will ensure future stability and peace of mind.

Affirmation & Gratitude

I make responsible financial decisions that bring peace, stability, and security into my life.

Cancer

25 December 2025

Dear Cancerian, creativity flows effortlessly today. Whether you're exploring new ideas or refining artistic projects, today's energy supports bold thinking and imagination. Let your creativity lead you toward fulfilling outcomes.

Affirmation & Gratitude

I embrace creativity in all its forms, knowing it brings joy and fulfillment to my life.

Cancer

26 December 2025

Dear Cancerian, relationships take focus today, with opportunities to strengthen your emotional bonds with loved ones through meaningful conversations. Be empathetic and open to understanding others. Today's energy favors emotional closeness.

Affirmation & Gratitude

I nurture my relationships with love, honesty, and empathy, creating deeper emotional connections with those I care about.

Cancer

27 December 2025

Dear Cancerian, career progress is highlighted today. The energy supports making bold, decisive steps toward your professional goals. Stay proactive and confident as you pursue new opportunities and expand your role.

Affirmation & Gratitude

I trust in my hard work and skills to guide me toward career success and personal growth.

Cancer

28 December 2025

Dear Cancerian, financial clarity is important today. Reassessing your long-term financial plans and making responsible decisions will ensure future stability. Practical choices made today will secure peace of mind.

Affirmation & Gratitude

I make thoughtful financial decisions that bring stability and peace to my future.

Cancer

29 December 2025

Dear Cancerian, creativity is heightened today, making it a great time to explore new artistic ideas or refine ongoing projects. Let your imagination guide you toward exciting possibilities. Creative expression will bring joy and satisfaction.

Affirmation & Gratitude

I trust in my creativity to bring new and fulfilling experiences into my life.

Cancer

30 December 2025

Dear Cancerian, relationships take center stage today. The cosmos encourages nurturing emotional connections with loved ones through open communication. Be present, empathetic, and kind, as today's energy favors emotional closeness and understanding.

Affirmation & Gratitude

I nurture my relationships with love, honesty, and gratitude, creating deeper emotional connections with those I cherish.

Cancer

31 December 2025

Dear Cancerian, career growth is in the spotlight today. The energy supports taking proactive steps toward your professional goals. Stay confident, motivated, and focused on long-term success as you pursue new challenges.

Affirmation & Gratitude

I trust in my hard work and dedication to guide me toward career success and fulfillment.

The Answers You Seek

Are Within

The "Daily Guidance" series offers an innovative approach to finding spiritual wisdom and practical advice. Each book in the series is a unique tool designed for daily introspection and decision-making. Readers are invited to meditate on a question or seek general guidance for the day, then flip to a random page in the book. The page they land on provides a personalized message from various spiritual sources, such as angels, tarot, or spirit animals. With each turn of the page, these books deliver insightful, positive messages and mantras to inspire personal growth and provide clarity on life's daily challenges and decisions.

Other books in this series:-

The Angelic Oracles
Daily Angel Tarot Reading
Mystic Tarot Cat
Oracle of the Tarot Cat
Vibes Unveiled
Spirit Animal Oracle
Answers from the Oracles
Messages from the Angels

Daily Guidance
SERIES